WITNESS TO
A Me

WITNESS TO PARTITION:
A Memoir

B.R. NANDA

Rupa & Co

First published 2003
Second impression 2006

Published by

Rupa & Co

7/16, Ansari Road, Daryaganj,
New Delhi 110 002

Sales Centres:

Allahabad Bangalore Chandigarh Chennai
Hyderabad Jaipur Kathmandu
Kolkata Mumbai Pune

Typeset in 12 pts Caxton by
Nikita Overseas Pvt. Ltd.
1410 Chiranjiv Tower
43 Nehru Place
New Delhi 110 019

Printed in India by
Gopsons Papers Ltd.
A-14 Sector 60
Noida 201 301

Contents

To the Reader

This book was written in December 1947 at Ferozepur, a border town on the newly created frontier between India and Pakistan. I had lived through the catastrophe which struck the Punjab in the months preceding and following the partition of India. What I saw in the West Punjab and later in the East Punjab shocked me and I decided to unburden myself in this book while the memories were fresh. It was published pseudonymously with the title *Punjab Uprooted* by Hind Kitabs, a Bombay publisher, in February 1948. Some of my friends who recently read the book told me that in view of the continuing public interest in the history of the partition, it would be of some value as an eye-witness account of what happened not only to the fast-diminishing members of the generation which underwent this traumatic experience, but to the wider public in our country today.

The book is being printed without any change in the original text, but I have written an introduction for this edition on the historical background, the underlying causes and the course of events which culminated in the partition of the subcontinent.

B.R. Nanda

16 May, 2003

Preface

I once read about a man who stood on the top of a hill and saw two passenger trains racing on a single track in opposite directions towards the inevitable disaster. During the last year, whenever I brooded on the communal strife in India, I thought of that passage and felt like that helpless man on the hill who was a witness to the tragedy which he could foresee but could not prevent.

At last, the terrific collision occurred. From the hill the accident appeared a great disaster, of which neither the causes nor the results were clear to those who were involved in it. Very many people were so busy in compiling death rolls in the two trains, in comparing the relative details of the wreckage, and in cursing the drivers and the passengers of the opposite train that they did not give a thought to the blunder of the station-master who had started the wrong train; they even forgot to tend the wounded, and to clear the debris in order to resume the journey.

The disaster of the Punjab is like a train accident; its story will be compiled by many historians from the versions of the drivers, the passengers and the passers-by, and from the death rolls certified by the nearest doctor. A few historians at least may go deeper into the causes of the accident, examine the rules of transportation and the mental outfit of the station-master.

In my analysis of the Punjab tragedy, I have given more attention to the deeper causes of the tension in the Punjab and to the forces which precipitated the actual outbreak than to the chronology or criminology of the period. If any reader hopes to find in this book statistics of murder, loot and arson or blood-curdling tales of atrocities he had better not start reading it. I could have culled a hundred hair-raising stories from the columns of the newspapers; I have myself heard moving stories of human suffering and guessed many more from faces mute with grief. But I have preferred to concentrate on the causes of the communal frenzy rather than on its manifestations. No amount of special pleading can excuse the violence on both sides of the border; yet these very people who ruthlessly cut human throats were only a few months earlier too peace-loving even to hit, just for the fun of it, a passing dog. That these people should have attacked and hounded out their compatriots in the name of religion and politics is a portent of some significance. The political-cum-religious movement, which inspired such violent emotions among protagonists and opponents and divided ancient neighbours by such gaping chasms, is a subject not only for political scientists but for psychologists. I was not writing a book on Pakistan, but insofar as the peace of the Punjab was upset by popular conceptions or mis-conceptions of Pakistan I had to take this political concept into account. The test of a political concept is not its legal or literal plausibility; not even the numerical support which it may secure, but its reduction to practice. Mr. Jinnah often reminds me of a magician who insisted upon the crowd to accept him as a *bona fide* magician before he would reveal the contents of his mysterious box, and when by sheer eloquence and will-power he had worn out the incredulity of the crowd, and opened his Pandora's box, what came out was a cobra which the magician would not control and which bit him as well as those who had at first declined to recognize the efficacy of his magic.

While dealing with the riots I have dealt with both the East Punjab and the West Punjab; this was inevitable because the events in the two parts of the Punjab have been reacting on each other and the violence could not have spread if news or rumours of happenings in one part had not provoked reaction and retaliation in the other part. In dealing with the problems of rehabilitation, I have confined myself to the East Punjab because I did not have sufficient first-hand data for the West Punjab; moreover, I am not sure that a national of India is expected to make suggestions on the problem of a *sovereign* state of Pakistan.

While writing on the subject of reconstruction of the East Punjab, I could not help looking beyond the provincial frontiers and putting provincial problems in the national setting; in their essentials the problems of moral and material reconstruction in all provinces are similar; only the symptoms in the East Punjab due to a sudden upheaval having become more pronounced call for a more urgent treatment. The East Punjab is the first severe test; if the Government and the people pass it successfully, the following tests elsewhere will be a child's play.

Introduction

The main theme of this book is the political earthquake which rocked the Punjab in 1947, leading to an estimated loss of one and a half million lives and migration of nearly five million Hindus and Sikhs from West Punjab to East Punjab and about the same number of Muslims from East Punjab to West Punjab across the newly-created border between India and Pakistan. When I wrote this book, I was mainly concerned with what had happened in the Punjab, but the epicentre of the political earthquake was not in Lahore, but in London, where the fateful decision for the partition of India was taken, and that decision itself was the outcome of, what Gandhi once described, 'three mighty conflicting forces of British imperialism, Congress nationalism and Muslim separatism.'[1] I propose to sketch in this chapter the origins, the underlying causes and the course of this triangular contest which resulted in the partition of the subcontinent.

1. Percy S. Gourgey, 'Indian Jews and the Indian Freedom Struggle' in *Indo-British Review*, Vol. XV, No. 1, p. 85.

It is more than fifty years since India was divided, but the origins and causes of the partition are still being keenly and even hotly debated. In Pakistan the popular—and the official—version is that the establishment of Pakistan was the fulfilment of the destiny of Indian Muslims. In India the partition of the subcontinent is regarded as a tragedy, which could have been averted; while Jinnah's crucial role is recognized, the Congress leaders, especially Nehru and Vallabhbhai Patel, have been blamed for errors of omission and commission which alienated the Muslim League. For example, Maulana Azad in his memoir, *India Wins Freedom,* argued that if Jawaharlal Nehru had agreed to concede two seats instead of one to the Muslim League for a coalition ministry in U.P. in 1937, or if he had not been indiscreet in his remarks on the Cabinet Mission Plan in his press conference at Bombay in July 1946, the situation may have been saved.

The indictment of Nehru, Patel and other Congress leaders does not bear critical scrutiny, and is largely based on wishful thinking. There has been a tendency to seek the causes of the partition in particular episodes during the months and years immediately preceding it. But in fact partition was the culmination of a movement of Muslim separatism which had been gathering strength at least since 1877 when the M.A.O. College was founded. Its founder, Syed Ahmad Khan, vigorously opposed the Indian National Congress when it was still in its infancy. Highly respected as he was as a religious and social reformer in his community, Syed Ahmad Khan threw his powerful influence in favour of isolation of the Muslims from the nationalist movement just when it started on its career. He raised the great question mark which was to shadow Indian politics during the next sixty years: what would be the position of the Muslim community in a free India? He put forward the idea which found wide acceptance among the Muslim elite of his day, that although fellow inhabitants of the Hindus and other communities, the Muslims in India constituted a nation separate from the rest and had their own special interests to protect and promote.

Syed Ahmad Khan has been hailed as a father-figure by Pakistani scholars. The political concept of Pakistan, as it was formulated by the Muslim League in 1940, was inconceivable in the last quarter of the nineteenth century. There was, however, much in the writings and speeches of Syed Ahmad Khan to nourish the psychology of Muslim separatism. That the Muslims, the former rulers of the subcontinent, had been the unjust victims of history, and especially of the events of 1857, that the Hindus had stolen a march over them in education and employment, that the Muslim youth must be educated separately from the Hindus under Muslim auspices, that for the Muslims to compete with the Hindus for entry into public services and elective bodies was a hopeless task, that any democratic polity must result in Hindu domination, that the British Raj was preferable to Hindu dominance inevitable in a representative form of government, were all assumptions of Syed Ahmad Khan, which became the dogmas of Muslim separatism during the next half a century.

The long rule of the Sultans of Delhi and the Mughal Emperors had ingrained in the Muslim elite of India a certain pride and faith in its destiny to rule over India, which seems to have survived the disintegration of the Mughal Empire and the advent of British rule. In his writings and speeches Syed Ahmad Khan made it a point to remind his co-religionists that they were the descendants of the former rulers of India. Twenty years later, in 1906, when an influential Muslim deputation, headed by the Aga Khan, waited on the Viceroy, Lord Minto, it pleaded for 'due consideration to be paid to the position which Muslims occupied in India a little more than a hundred years ago and of which the traditions have naturally not faded from their minds'. Lord Minto, in his reply to the deputation, was chivalrous enough to greet them as 'the descendants of a conquering and ruling race'. This self-image of the Muslim elite as the former rulers of India became a block in the way of the Muslim elite in identifying itself with the Indian National Congress. The signatories of the memorial to Minto described themselves as 'nobles, jagirdars, taluqdars, zamindars, lawyers, merchants and others'. Consisting as it did largely of the titled and landed gentry, with a sprinkling of professional classes and retired government servants, the Muslim elite by no means was a monolithic group; it had its sub-divisions of Sunnis and Shias, Mughals and Syeds, Rajputs and so on. But in its political orientation, in its loyalty to the British Raj and in its obsession with the spectre of 'Hindu domination', it was a fairly coherent group. Most of its members were apolitical, not really interested in politics; they were happy enough with the status quo and the patronage of British officials. The political demands of the Indian National Congress, such as the Indianization of the higher services, equitable financial burdens between India and Britain, reduction in military expenditure, reduction in land revenue, the separation of executive and judiciary, did not excite them. The mindset of the Muslim elite suited the British bureaucracy, which came to look upon the Muslim community—as it did upon the landlords and the princes—as pillars of the British Raj. When the joint effort of Muslim League politicians and the Anglo-Indian lobby in London succeeded in injecting separate electorates into the Minto-Morley reforms in 1909, Lovat Fraser, the editor of the British-owned *The Times of India,* confided to Dunlop-Smith, the Private Secretary to the Viceroy: 'Men like the Aga Khan plainly feel that in pressing for large separate treatment for Mohammedans, they are fighting our battle much more than their own. We have far more to lose than the Muslims by an entente between Islam and Hinduism.'[2]

The British knew what they were doing, but they needed allies to checkmate the Indian National Congress. Ironically, the bluntest comment on separate electorates is to be found in an official document, the joint report of the Viceroy, Lord Chelmsford, and Secretary of State Edwin Montagu, which formed the basis of the Reforms Act of 1919:

2. Martin Gilbert, *Servant of India* (London, 1966), p. 202.

Division by creeds and classes means the creation of political camps organized against each other, and teaches men to think as partisans and not as citizens; and it is difficult to see how the change from this system to national representation is ever to occur. The British Government is often accused of dividing men in order to govern them. But if it unnecessarily divides them at the very moment when it proposes to start them on the road to governing themselves, it will find it difficult to meet the charge of being hypocritical or shortsighted.

This paragraph seems to have been drafted by Montagu, one of the most liberal and sympathetic of British ministers, who had presided over the India Office in London. It did not represent the policy of the British bureaucracy in India or of the Anglo-Indian lobby in England whose view was succinctly expressed by Secretary of State Birkenhead to the then Viceroy Lord Reading in 1925: 'The more it is made obvious that their [Hindu and Muslim] antagonisms are profound and immense and affect irreconcilable sections of the population, the more conspicuously is the fact illustrated that we and we alone can play the part of the composers.'

II

The question of safeguards for the Muslim community in the constitutional reforms began with the incorporation of separate electorates in the electoral system in 1909. The Congress, led by the great Parsi leaders, Dadabhai Naoroji and Pherozeshah Mehta, and Gopal Krishna Gokhale, was quick to detect in them the thin end of the wedge, which would ultimately pull the two major communities asunder. But seven years later, the Congress itself reversed its policy under the leadership of B.G. Tilak, who believed that by conceding the Muslim demands in toto he was helping to solve the communal problem for good. Jinnah, who was one of the chief architects of the Lucknow Pact in 1916 and presided over the Muslim League session in that year, evidently held the same belief, because he frankly acknowledged in his presidential address the 'ungrudging spirit in which the Hindu leaders had recognized and met the Muslim communal position'. 'I rejoice to think,' he added, 'that a final settlement has at last been reached which sets the seal on Hindu-Muslim cooperation.'

The Congress leaders made themselves believe that the Lucknow Pact was a 'final settlement' of the political differences between the two communities. Little did they know that there was going to be no final settlement as there was going to be no fixity in Muslim demands. For one thing, it was not easy to reconcile the claims of all the communities and parties for weightage in legislatures and jobs. For another, there was a fundamental difference between the objectives of the two main political parties. The objective of the Congress was to end foreign rule and to create a united front to fight it. The leaders of the Muslim League were interested neither in hastening the end of the British Raj nor in embroiling themselves with it; they had more limited and practical concerns with power and patronage in their provinces. In a letter dated 28 May 1937 to Jinnah, the philosopher-poet Sir Mohammed Iqbal, described the All India Muslim League as a body of the upper classes of Indian Muslims, not of the masses, whose chief preoccupation was with securing posts for their sons, relatives and friends. Jinnah was not unaware of the character of the feudal and titled gentry with whom and through whom he had to work; he once said they included some 'spineless people who whatever they may say to me will consult the [British] Deputy Commissioner about what they should do.'[3]

The idea that in legislatures of self-governing India all Hindu members would vote *en bloc* on political issues was absurd, but the fear of 'Hindu domination' had been firmly planted in the psyche of the Muslim elite since the days of Syed Ahmad Khan. The demands for safeguards went on escalating over the years, until, with Jinnah's Fourteen Points in 1929, they included every possible claim which could have been advanced vis-a-vis the Hindus within the framework of the representative system of government. In 1932 the Communal Award pronounced by Ramsay MacDonald, the Prime Minister of England, under pressure from the Government of India, conceded virtually all the Muslim demands, but the problem was not solved. The Muslim

3. S.M. Ikram, *Modern Muslim India and the Birth of Pakistan* (Lahore, 1970), pp. 356-7.

political elite's obsession with the demographic reality of a three-fourths Hindu majority in India remained. What was needed was a formula in constitutional arithmetic to offset the Hindu majority at the centre in a future constitution for India and to prove $25 = 75$. This formula was produced by Rahmat Ali, a student in Cambridge, who, in a pamphlet *Now or Never*, published in 1933, propounded the 'two-nation theory' and its corollary, the establishment of Pakistan, as an independent Muslim State consisting of Muslim-majority provinces in the north-west and north-east.

Pakistani historians have attributed the Muslim opposition to Indian nationalism from the days of Syed Ahmad Khan to the sentiment of 'Muslim nationalism'. Now, the term 'Muslim nationalism' makes as little sense as 'Christian nationalism' or 'Buddhist nationalism'. Basic to nationalism is its relationship to a specific country or region. Not until the emergence of the concept of Pakistan in the mid-thirties did such a possible relationship emerge, and Muslim separatism in India begin to acquire characteristics of secessionism and nationalism. In the words of S.R. Mehrotra, the historian of the Indian National Congress, it was 'an accident of geography', the existence of Muslim-majority regions in the north-west and north-east, which brought the idea of Pakistan into the domain of practical politics. If the Muslim population of India had been evenly distributed throughout the country, it would have been a minority everywhere, which could neither have willed nor been in a position to dominate any region.

By the mid-thirties, the concept of Pakistan was being debated by Muslim politicians. Sir Mohammed Iqbal argued at the Third Round Table Conference (1933) that the Muslims did not want to have any central government in India because it was bound to be dominated by the Hindus. Two years later, the Aga Khan wrote to Sir Fazl-i-Husain that the only safety for Muslims in India lay in working for the achievement of Pakistan.[4] Bimal Prasad has recently argued that Jinnah had been converted to the idea of Pakistan by 1937 but deliberately did not reveal it.[5] He quotes from a letter written by Lord Brabourne, the Governor of Bombay, to the Viceroy, Lord Linlithgow, in June 1937 that Jinnah told him that he was 'planning to consolidate the Muslim League throughout India. His policy is to preach communalism morning, noon and night and teach [the Muhammadans] generally to stand on their own feet and make themselves independent of the Hindus.'

Jinnah's conversion to the ultimate stage in Muslim separatism was to prove a turning point not only in his own political career, but in the history of India.

III

Jinnah was 61 in 1937. In his youth, he had come under the influence of Dadabhai Naoroji and Gokhale and taken to law and politics. In his early forties, he was

4. Waheed Ahmad, Aga Khan to Fazl-i-Husain, 13 August 1935 in *Letters of Mian Fazl-i-Husain* (Lahore, 1976) pp. 429-35.
5. Bimal Prasad, *Pathway to India's Partition*, Vol. II, p. 406.

a front-rank politician, and took a prominent part in the negotiation of the Lucknow Pact in 1916, which brought the Indian National Congress and the All India Muslim League on a common platform. Those were the days when he was hailed as a nationalist and 'ambassador of Hindu-Muslim unity'. He left the Congress when it accepted Gandhi's leadership in 1920. In 1918 he was at the centre of the national stage; two years later he found himself in political limbo. Several other veteran leaders of the Congress, such as Surendranath Banerjea, Annie Besant, D.E. Wacha and Tej Bahadur Sapru, had a similar experience, which was due to the intensity with which Gandhi's personality and politics appealed to millions of Indians who had so far been unaffected by politics. Jinnah never forgave Gandhi for his humiliation.

Ousted from the Congress, Jinnah fell back on the All India Muslim League; he became its 'permanent president', but his hold on it remained somewhat shaky. At the Round Table Conference in London, 1930-31, he found himself utterly alone. Marginalized in Indian politics, he decided to settle down in England to practise at the English Bar. When he returned to India to lead the Muslim League at the first general election under the new constitution in 1935, he pleaded for a Hindu-Muslim, and indeed a Congress-League, accord. He formed a Parliamentary Board of the All India Muslim League and toured the country from one end to the other, but the results of the 1937 elections came as a great blow to him. The League secured less than five per cent of the Muslim votes. It won 39 out of 117 Muslim seats in Bengal, but only one seat in the Punjab out of 84 Muslim seats, and three in Sind out of 33 Muslim seats. It did not win a single Muslim seat in the provincial legislatures of Bihar, NWFP, Central Provinces and Orissa. In Madras it won ten seats, in Bombay twenty. In the U.P. it won 27 out of 64 Muslim seats in a House of 228 members while the Congress won 133 seats. With this poor showing, the League hardly qualified for a coalition with the Congress in most of the provinces. Only in one province, that is, in U.P., there were serious negotiations for a coalition. The Congress has been criticized for spurning a coalition with the Muslim League in U.P., which is alleged to have fanned the fires of Muslim frustration, which in turn fuelled the movement for Pakistan. In his incisive analysis of this issue, S.R. Mehrotra (*Towards India's Freedom,* p. 226) has exposed some of the persistent myths on the failure of negotiations between the Congress and the League in U.P. He describes the assertion of Maulana Azad in his autobiography that if the Congress had been generous enough to offer one more seat to the Muslims League in the U.P. Cabinet in 1937, the Muslim League party in the province would have disintegrated and there would have been no demand for Pakistan, as 'too naive to merit consideration.' The fact is that some negotiations did take place between the Congress and some local League members of the legislature headed by Khaliquzzaman, an ex-Congressman, but they failed to produce any positive result. There is evidence to indicate that Khaliquzzaman was seriously thinking of joining the Congress along with his supporters. Jinnah was so perturbed by this possibility that he came to Lucknow in May 1937 and took the chair at a meeting of the U.P. Muslim League Parliamentary Board to decide the terms for a coalition with the Congress. He made it clear that he would not permit any local piecemeal agreement with the Congress. His approach to coalitions became clear in the course of some informal exchanges with Congress leadership on the inclusion of Muslim League legislators in the Congress ministry in Bombay. He insisted that his nominees would neither join the Congress legislature party nor accept its discipline and the principle of joint responsibility of the cabinet. The Congress leaders had thus reasons to fear that if the League members were taken into Congress ministries on such terms, Jinnah would dictate the whole policy of the government through his nominees.

Whatever the rationale behind the final decision of the Congress leadership, there is no doubt that it created a feeling of grievance on which Jinnah mounted a massive propaganda offensive to alienate his co-religionists of both Muslim-minority and Muslim-majority provinces from the Congress and to rally them under his leadership.

In the summer of 1937, Jinnah was faced with the stark realities of Indian politics. His hopes of making the League the representative organization of the Muslim community under his leadership to enable him to negotiate with the Congress on equal terms had been dashed to the ground. His party scarcely figured on the political map of India under the new constitution. While Gandhi and Nehru were to guide and control six (and later, eight) out of eleven provincial ministries, there was not a single ministry he could call his own. It may have seemed that he could do little about it until the time came for the next general elections. He was, however, not the man to let history pass over his head. 'In politics', he once said, 'one has to play one's game on the chessboard.'[6] He made a masterly move calculated to achieve through a propaganda blast what the ballot box had denied him. The by-election to the Jhansi-Jalaun-Hamirpur Muslim seat in U.P. (June-July 1937) gave an inkling of his new strategy. He appealed to the voters in the name of Allah and the Holy Koran to support the Muslim League candidate. In October 1937 at the Lucknow session of the All India Muslim League, religious fervour rose to a high pitch. Not even three months had passed since the Congress formed its ministries, but Jinnah was already proclaiming that Muslims could not expect 'any justice or fair play at their hands'.[7]

What was this Congress tyranny against which Jinnah was raising a hue and cry. One of the grievances was

6. Waheed Ahmad, *Quaid-i-Azam Mohamed Ali Jinnah, The Nation's Voice, Speeches and Statements, March 1935-March 1946* (Karachi, 1992), p. 332.
7. Jamil-ud-Din Ahmad, *Some Recent Speeches and Writings of Mr. Jinnah* (Lahore, 1946), p. 30.

that excessive reverence was paid to Gandhi and his birthday had been declared a holiday. 'To declare my birthday as a holiday', commented Gandhi, 'should be classified as a cognizable offence.' Another grievance was the display of the Congress flag on government buildings. The Congress flag was born during the days of the Khilafat movement, and its colours had been determined to represent the various communities: saffron for the Hindus, green for the Muslims and white for other minorities. Objections were raised to the *Bande Mataram* song on the ground that its original context in a novel by the nineteenth-century Bengal novelist, Bankimchandra Chatterji, had communal overtones. The song had first become popular during the agitation against the partition of Bengal, when it came to be regarded by the British as a symbol of sedition. The song had been sung at Congress meetings at which Jinnah himself had been present. Nevertheless, out of deference to Muslim susceptibilities, the Congress Working Committee decided in 1937 that only the first two stanzas should be sung on ceremonial occasions. Gandhi's advice to Congressmen was not to sing the *Bande Mataram* or hoist the Congress flag if a single Muslim objected.

One of the targets of the League's criticism was the Wardha Scheme of Basic Education which had been devised largely by two eminent Muslim educationists, Dr. Zakir Husain and K.G. Saiyidain, to substitute a coordinated training in the use of the hand and the eye for a notoriously bookish and volatile learning which village children unlearned after leaving school.

The British Governors of Congress-ruled provinces took notice of these allegations and reported to Lord Linlithgow, the Viceroy, that the Congress ministries had been, on the whole, impartial and fair to the Muslim community. Sir Harry Haig, the Governor of U.P., in his letter of 23 March 1938, wrote that the attacks of the Muslim League on the U.P. Ministry were 'very unfair' and the allegations were marked by 'deliberate falsity to a degree which even the manoeuvres of politics can hardly excuse'.[8] The Governor of Bihar, Sir Maurice Hallett, commenting on the allegations of the League, wrote on 6 January 1939 that from his experience both in Bihar and U.P. he 'did not see any orders were passed by the Congress ministry that were really detrimental to Muslim interests.'[9] Sir Francis Wylie, the Governor of Central Provinces and Berar, told the Viceroy (22 June 1939) that the 'accusations of gross anti-Muslim bias' against the Congress government were 'moonshine'.[10]

Jinnah rejected the proposal of the Congress President, Rajendra Prasad, that Sir Maurice Gwyer, Chief Justice of the Federal Court, be asked to hold an inquiry into the League's allegations. The fact was that Jinnah was not interested in judicial inquiries; his object was not to convince the British or the Hindus, but to rouse the deepest fears of his own community. The cry of 'Islam in danger', the reiteration of 'Congress tyranny',

8. Linlithgow Papers
9. Ibid.
10. Ibid.

and the spectre of 'Hindu Raj' widened the communal gulf and created the climate in which the proposal for the partition of India could be mooted. He propounded the two-nation theory: that India was not one nation, that the Muslims of India constituted a separate nation from the Hindus, and that they were entitled to a separate homeland of their own. In March 1940, this theory was embodied in the resolution of the All India Muslim League at its Lahore session, which declared that no constitutional plan for India would be workable or acceptable to Muslims in India unless it was based on a demarcation of Muslim-majority areas in the north-west and north-east as independent states.

IV

The Pakistan resolution, as it came to be known, passed by the Muslim League gave a new twist to the communal problem. All the solutions hitherto thought of—separate electorates, composite cabinets, reservation of posts—suddenly became out of date. The demand for an independent Muslim state came as a bombshell not only to Congressmen but to almost everyone outside the inner circles of the League. Abul Kalam Azad described it as 'meaningless and absurd'. Sir Sikander Hayat Khan, Premier of the Punjab, rejected outright the idea of the partition of India. The British authorities considered it as a bargaining counter to extract a better deal from the Congress. Thus in 1940 the concept of Pakistan seemed a political phantom. Seven years later it had become a reality.

Of the magnitude of Jinnah's achievement there is no doubt. In just ten years, he brought the All India Muslim League from a total eclipse to a position where it decisively influenced the course of events. The League had been the principal carrier of Muslim separatism in Indian politics since its inception in 1906; but until the early thirties it was a moribund party. It was Jinnah's new strategy which gave it a new lease of life. Iskander Mirza, who rose to be the President of Pakistan, told a British historian that towards the end of Jinnah's life when someone praised the contribution of the Muslim League to the winning of Pakistan, Jinnah remarked, 'Do not talk about the Muslim League; I and my stenographer created Pakistan.'[11]

With his well-timed and pungent speeches and press statements Jinnah was able to rouse his co-religionists and to keep the Congress at bay. By working up religious emotion, by skirting the details of his demand for Pakistan, by concentrating on a tirade against 'Hindu Raj' and 'Congress tyranny', and by keeping his cards close to his chest, he was able to keep his following in good order. Each of his followers could see Pakistan in his own image. The orthodox looked forward to a state which would reproduce the purity of pristine Islam; those with a secular outlook hoped for tangible benefits; the Muslim middle class, which had been left behind

11. Quoted by S.R. Mehrotra in 'The Creation of Pakistan: The Triumph and Tragedy of Jinnah' in *Indian Archives,* January-December 1977, pp. 75-92.

in the race for plums of government service, trade and industry by the Hindus, was attracted by the idea of a Muslim state. Muslim landlords were relieved at the prospect of deliverance from 'progressive' and socialist politicians like Nehru who indulged in the dangerous talk of abolishing zamindari. And such was the magical effect of Jinnah's propaganda that his adherents in the Punjab and Bengal failed to see that the very logic which justified the division of India could be applied to the partition of the Punjab and Bengal.

Jinnah's success in building up the Muslim League was due not only to his undoubted polemical and tactical skills, but also to the tension between the Congress and the Government which prevailed throughout this period. The outbreak of the Second World War came as a god-send to him. The breach between the Congress and the Government and the resignation of Congress ministries left the field clear for the League's propaganda for Pakistan. Having written off the Congress, the Viceroy and his advisers could not resist the temptation of supporting its principal opponent. The Viceroy's declaration of August 1940 gave Jinnah a virtual veto on constitutional advance. Two years later, the Cripps Mission gave the Muslim-majority provinces the option of seceding from the future Indian Union. While the Congress was outlawed, the British Governors went out of their way to install Muslim League ministries in Sind, NWFP and Assam. In 1945 Lord Wavell allowed the Simla conference called for the formation of an Interim Government to fail because Jinnah would not let any non-League Muslim to be included in it. In 1946, the Cabinet Mission Plan, after rejecting Pakistan in theory, produced a three-tier constitution in which the League professed to recognize 'the ultimate foundation for Pakistan'.

From 1937 onwards, Jinnah made unabashed appeal to religious beliefs and prejudices for political ends. In December 1938, the Council of All India Muslim League passed a resolution asking ulemas to issue fatwas warning Muslims against joining the Congress; the fatwas were to be published under the authority of the Muslim League and propagated among Friday congregations in the mosques in towns and villages. When Nehru returned after a brief visit to Europe in 1938, he was struck by the similarity between the propaganda methods of the Muslim League in India and the Nazis in Germany.

> The League leaders had begun to echo the Fascist tirade against democracy. ... Nazis were wedded to a negative policy. So also was the League. The League was anti-Hindu, anti-Congress, and anti-national. ... The Nazis raised the cry of hatred against the Jews, the League [had] raised [its] cry against the Hindus.[12]

The appeal in the name of Islam reached its culmination in the general elections of 1945-46. In her latest book *Self and Sovereignty*, Ayesha Jalal tells us about meetings in the North-West Frontier Province in

12. Dorothy Norman, *Nehru, The First Sixty Years*, Vol. II, pp. 344-5.

which appeals to vote for the Muslim League were made 'in the name of Allah and the Prophet.'[13] The services of pirs and heads of religious shrines were requisitioned to warn Muslims in rural areas to vote for the League or face ostracism. Through constant reiteration of dangers of 'Hindu Raj' and 'Congress tyranny' a fear psychosis was induced in the Muslim masses. This tactic paid rich dividends to the Muslim League. It won all the 30 Muslim seats in the Central Assembly and 439 out of 490 Muslim seats in the provincial assemblies. It had fought the elections on the issue of Pakistan and won a landslide victory. At last, Jinnah had the mandate he needed for the negotiations for the transfer of power from British to Indian hands which began with the arrival of the Cabinet Mission in March 1946.

V

The negotiations with the Cabinet Mission brought Jinnah to the negotiating table and compelled him to spell out his terms. In one important respect the political situation was changing. The rift between the Congress and the Government which had all along given the Muslim League a favourable bargaining position was closing. The leaders of the League seemed to sense it. From the beginning of 1946, they started harping on dangers of a civil war if their demands were not conceded. In March 1946, Abdur Rab Nishtar, later a

13. Ayesha Jalal, *Self and Sovereignty* (London, 2000), p. 468.

League nominee to the Interim Government, declared: 'The real fact is that Mussalmans belong to a martial race and are no believers in non-violent principles of Mr. Gandhi.'[14] Abdul Qaiyum Khan, the League leader of N.W.F.P., pointed out that the people in the tribal areas, 'who were all armed', were for Pakistan. Sir Feroz Khan Noon threatened that if Muslims were placed 'under one central government or Hindu Raj, then the havoc which the Muslims will play will put to shame what Chengiz Khan and Halaku did.'[15]

The triangular negotiations between the British Cabinet Mission, the Congress and the League failed and the Cabinet Mission Plan was stillborn. In July 1946, Viceroy Lord Wavell invited Nehru and Jinnah as leaders of the Congress and the League respectively to form an Interim Government. Jinnah's conditions were not acceptable to the Viceroy, who then decided to form a government with the Congress alone headed by Nehru. Jinnah was furious. He announced 16 August 1946 would be observed as the 'Direct Action Day'. 'This day we bid goodbye to constitutional methods', he told the League Council, 'today we have also forged a pistol and are ready to use it.' On that day communal riots began in Calcutta which took a toll of at least 5,000 lives besides more than 10,000 injured. Two months later, disturbances broke out in the Muslim-majority district of Noakhali in East Bengal in which local hooligans

14. *Dawn,* 26 March 1946
15. *The Indian Annual Register,* January-June 1946, pp. 196-97.

burnt property of Hindus, looted their crops and desecrated their temples. There were also shocking reports of forcible conversions and kidnapping of Hindu women. The communal riots spread like a chain reaction from Calcutta to East Bengal, from East Bengal to Bihar and from Bihar to West Punjab.

This communal violence, in its scale and intensity, was in an entirely different category from the local riots on such issues as cow-slaughter and music before the mosques. Gandhi undertook walking tours through the riot-torn areas of Bengal and Bihar. The Congress leaders condemned the riots and called for stern action. Unfortunately, the League leaders reacted with a political rather than a human bias. Even though a League ministry was in office in Calcutta, Jinnah blamed the riots on 'Gandhi, the Viceroy and the British'; each communal riot was cited as a further endorsement of the two-nation theory and of the inevitability of the partition of India. George Abell, the Private Secretary to Lord Wavell, after a meeting with Jinnah's deputy, Nawabzada Liaquat Ali Khan, on 18th November 1946, got a 'clear impression that the League could not afford to let communal feeling in the country to die down.'[16]

Shaken by the riots, Lord Wavell inducted the Muslim League into the Interim Government, but with results which were just the opposite of what he had hoped for. The Interim Government, instead of becoming more

16. George Abell to Wavell, 18 November 1946 in N. Mansergh and P. Moon (ed.), *The Transfer of Power*, Vol. IX (London, 1980), No. 49.

representative and effective, was paralysed by the conflict between the two political parties. The Viceroy did not have a clue as to what he should do, and proposed a 'breakdown' plan for the evacuation of British military forces from the subcontinent province by province. Prime Minister Attlee considered it a counsel of despair, and decided to appoint a new Viceroy to devise and implement a scheme for a more orderly termination of British rule.

On 20 February 1947, the British Government issued a momentous statement announcing its definite intention to take necessary steps to effect transfer of power into responsible Indian hands by a date not later than June 1948. This statement could well have acted as a shock therapy to bring the contending political parties together. It had just the opposite effect because of the provision in it that if on the appointed date (30 June 1948) there was no single government for the whole of the country, the British Government might transfer power in some areas to 'existing provincial governments or in some such other ways as may seem reasonable.' The Muslim League which had its ministries only in Bengal and Sind took this to mean that it had just 15 months to capture provincial governments in the remaining provinces, Punjab, NWFP and Assam, which it claimed for Pakistan. It launched 'direct action' in the form of demonstrations, which resulted in widespread and serious communal disturbances in West Punjab in March 1947. The response of the Congress Working Committee came in a resolution demanding partition of the Punjab; it was a signal to the Muslim League that it would not be allowed to get away with the Hindu-majority districts of the Punjab and Bengal if it insisted on the secession of Muslim-majority areas in the east and west. After all, the logic which the Muslim League applied to the partition of India could as well justify the partition of these two provinces.

Thus even before Lord Mountbatten arrived in India at the end of March, the Congress leadership was reconciling itself to Pakistan as 'a lesser evil'. The choice was narrowing down to partition or civil war. Nehru and Vallabhbhai Patel had been chastened by their experience in the Interim Government and the growing lawlessness in the country. A *modus vivendi* with the League seemed not remote, but impossible. Partition of India was bad enough, but even worse possibilities had begun to loom up. The princely rulers of western and central India under the inspiration of rulers of larger states, such as the Nawab of Bhopal, were thinking in terms of 'leagues of princes'. It was the intrigue by the ruler of Bastar, a small state in central India, with the Nizam of Hyderabad, and the attitude of the Political Department to it which finally convinced Vallabhbhai Patel that it was imperative to secure immediate British withdrawal even if it meant acceptance of partition of India. Nehru arrived at the same conclusion after his frustrating experience in the Interim Government where he noticed 'a mental alliance' between the British officers and the leaders of the League.

It was the considered view of Prof. N. Mansergh, who edited the twelve volumes of the *Transfer of Power 1942-47,* that it was the threat by the Muslim League that a 'civil war more terrible than any in the history of Asia would ensue', if power was not transferred to two successor states, which made any other settlement seem impracticable to the British Government in 1947.[17] Insofar as the Muslim League's strategy of threatening a civil war and anarchy was designed to rouse the Muslims, frighten the Hindus, and impress the British, it succeeded. Pakistani writers are unanimous in lauding Jinnah's tactical skill and inflexible will, his determination to achieve a sovereign Muslim State. One wonders, however, whether Jinnah had really thought through his cherished project and its possible human cost.

'Two nations, Mr. Jinnah,' Edward Thompson, a British writer, asked him in 1939 'confronting each other in every province? Every town? Every village?'

'Two nations', replied the Quaid-i-Azam, 'confronting each other, in every province, every town, every village. That is the only solution.'

'That is a very terrible solution, Mr. Jinnah,' said Thompson. 'It is a terrible solution', replied the Quaid-i-Azam, 'but it is the only one.'[18]

17. Diana Mansergh (ed.), *Independence Years, The Selected Indian and Commonwealth Papers of Prof. Nicholos Mansergh* (New Delhi, 1999), pp. 60-61.
18. Edward Thompson, *Enlist India for Freedom* (London, 1940), pp. 51-52.

Jinnah paid no heed to Edward Thompson's warning in 1939. Twenty years later, a western writer, Kenneth Cragg, questioning the logic of the idea of Pakistan, wrote, 'it was created, on a plea of self-determination on behalf of some 24 per cent of all India (that is the Muslims), while itself enclosing from Hindu India a non-Muslim minority of 40 per cent. Thus it does greater violence to its own principle than does the India from which it seceded, and in doing so in the thousands of square miles where Hindus, Sikhs and Muslims lived in closest intermingling, unofficial warfare routed ten million people from their homes and brought sharp economic distress, disintegration of the social fabric and the near-downfall of the new governments. It was a sanguinary climax, on behalf of a State in two halves, partitioning both the Punjab and Bengal, with no historical frontiers, and racially no more homogeneous than a united India. ... "As an article of faith," said the Quaid-i-Azam, "Pakistan is a matter of life and death." He was right: there was death in the counsel as well as life.'[19]

VI

In the post-partition period while the establishment of Pakistan is considered a fulfilment of the Muslim nationalism and a feather in Jinnah's cap, there has

19. Kenneth Cragg, *Counsels in Contemporary Islam* (Edinburgh, 1965), pp. 23-25.

been a tendency in India to view the partition as an avoidable tragedy. Several questions have continued to gnaw at the minds of the Indian intelligentsia. Could the Congress leaders have done more to conciliate Jinnah and to satisfy the doubts and demands of the Muslim minority about the constitution of independent India? Alternatively, why did the Congress leaders, especially Nehru and Patel, not accept Gandhi's advice and oppose partition to the bitter end? And finally, why did Gandhi not resort to the ultimate weapon, such as a fast to prevent the partition of the country?

The answer to the first question is that between 1937 and 1947, the Congress did try to mend its fences with Jinnah, but without any success. From 1937 to 1940, he refused to begin a dialogue with the Congress until it conceded the League's exclusive right to represent the Muslim community. From 1940 onwards, he refused to begin a dialogue until the Congress conceded the principle of the partition of India. While he did not budge an inch from the position he had adopted in 1940, the Congress was continually softening its stand under the impact of strident propaganda by the League and the confrontation with the Government. In 1942, the Congress Working Committee passed a resolution on the Cripps proposals which declared that it 'cannot think in terms of compelling people of any territorial unit to remain in the Indian Union against their declared and established will.' In 1944, in his talks with Jinnah, Gandhi not only accepted the principle of the partition of the country, but even discussed the mechanism for effecting it, but Jinnah rejected his plea that some connection should remain between the two countries after the partition. And finally, in the summer of 1946, the Congress accepted after much heart-searching a constitution with a three-tier structure and a weak centre limited to only three subjects—foreign affairs, defence and communications. When such a proposal was suggested for the two wings of Pakistan in 1970, Z.A. Bhutto compared the lot of such a government to that of 'a widow without a pension'.

Jinnah did not respond to these changes in the attitude of the Congress. Every overture was rejected, every concession was treated as a bargaining counter for a better deal. Only once in 1946 he seemed to agree to a compromise when he accepted the Cabinet Mission Plan, but his acceptance was more apparent than real. In its resolution (6 June 1946) the Muslim League Council saw in the Cabinet Mission Plan 'the basis and foundation of Pakistan'. Clearly, the League did not consider the Cabinet Mission Plan as a final compromise between the Congress ideal of a strong and united India and the League's objective of two separate sovereign states. Jinnah himself made no secret of his hope that the Cabinet Mission Plan would be a stepping stone towards an independent Pakistan. Even this ambiguous acceptance was revoked after seven weeks. While Jinnah's position in negotiations had little room for flexibility, his political style was hardly calculated to assist a compromise. He heaped invective and ridicule on Congress leaders, from Gandhi and Nehru downwards. After the abortive Gandhi-Jinnah talks, Jinnah, in a press conference on 4 October 1944, described the Mahatma's assertions 'dangerous, tortuous and crooked'.[20]

As we have already seen, Congress leaders had been chastened by their experience of working with the Muslim League in the Interim Government as well as by the growing lawlessness in the country. The choice seemed to them between anarchy and the partition. They resigned themselves to the latter in order to salvage three-fourth of India from the chaos which threatened the whole. The decision was not that of only Nehru and Patel. In the meeting of the All India Congress Committee, 157 voted for it and only 15 against it.

Gandhi had been desperately wanting to pull the country back from the precipice. In the first week of April 1947 when he met Mountbatten, he suggested that Jinnah should be invited to form a government of his own choice to which the Congress would extend its support. The proposal 'astounded' the Viceroy; it was rejected out of hand by Nehru and Patel who were certain that such unilateral gestures would not melt Jinnah's heart. Mountbatten did not convey Gandhi's proposal to Jinnah, but it is doubtful whether the League leader's reaction would have been very different from what he had said about a similar proposal made by the Mahatma in August 1942:[21]

20. *Dawn*, 5 October 1944
21. Jamil-ud-Din Ahmad, *Recent Speeches and Writings of Mr. Jinnah* (Lahore, 1940), p. 447.

If they [the Congress] are sincere I should welcome it. If the British Government accepts the solemn recommendation of Mr. Gandhi and by an arrangement hands over the government of the country to the Muslim League, I am sure that under Muslim rule non-Muslims would be treated fairly, justly, nay, generously; and further the British will be making full amends to the Muslims by restoring the government of India to them from whom they had taken it.

After Gandhi's proposal to hand over power to Jinnah did not find favour, he put forward a basic proposition that there must be peace before there was Pakistan. His proposal that the British had no right to partition India but should leave India to her fate was acceptable neither to the Muslims nor to the British. With the looming threat of a civil war, the Labour Government could hardly afford to leave India, as Gandhi said, to its fate. Such a momentous decision as the winding up of the British Empire in India needed the support of public opinion and the approval of both Houses of Parliament in Britain. Churchill and the Conservative Party would have never endorsed a solution which had not been accepted by Jinnah and the Muslim League.

To prevent partition, there was no point in Gandhi's launching civil disobedience against the British, who were not susceptible to such moral pressures, and were in any case leaving the country. Nor would there have been any point in his undertaking a fast in West Punjab or East Bengal where he had been painted for years as an enemy of Islam. The leaders of the Muslim League were proof against the nuances of satyagraha; they would at once have denounced Gandhi's fast as a trick to cheat them of the prize of Pakistan which lay within their grasp.

The Muslim League had insisted that there could be no peace in India until its demand for the creation of a separate Muslim state was conceded. The Mountbatten Plan of June 1947, which provided for two new Dominions to come into existence from 15 August 1947, conceded this demand. After its acceptance by the British Government, the Indian National Congress and the All India Muslim League, the plan was expected to usher in an era of communal amity in the subcontinent. What actually ensued, however, was violence on an unprecedented scale as we shall observe in the following pages.

Chapter I

Insurance against Anarchy

It was Christmas eve, 1946. As I sipped my cup of hot tea off a crowded table in the 'Lorangs' at Lahore, I could not help catching the air of abandonment in the restaurant and outside. There was much shuffling of feet as customers filed in and out. Inside the hall, to the accompaniment of the usual music, a multitude of voices were fused into a confused and noisy gaiety. The crowded road, the thronged restaurant, the rippling laughter of pretty women in prettier clothes—this was the customary life of the gay town of Lahore. A Muslim friend, a journalist, sat next to me. Our conversation inevitably rambled into politics. As we recalled (in the *Statesman's* gruesome coinage) the Great Calcutta Killing, the Noakhali tragedy, and the Bihar frenzy, we could not hide our satisfaction at the continued peace in our Province. 'The Punjabi character,' said my friend, 'is incapable of such things. A Punjabi may have fits of violent anger, but he is as open as his anger is short-lived'. He appeared to set much store by the Punjabis' 'sturdy commonsense' to which the paid publicity agents of the Punjab Government appealed in prepared speeches. 'How long will this peace last?' he asked. 'As long as Sir Khizr remains in office', I replied. My friend burst into derisive laughter.

I was not surprised. During the last many years the Unionists had been discussed with amused tolerance in thinking circles. The successive ministries had been admittedly conservative, corrupt and in many ways inefficient; they had been supported by a Co-operative Vested Interest Society in which every member of the ministerial party held preference shares. Sir Sikandar's tradition of parliamentary management was reminiscent of the bad old days of Walpole's England. Every Honourable Member had his price. It was a frank, and sometimes, a fair distribution of loaves and fishes. Sir Sikandar spent much of his time in rewarding faithful followers and buying off potential rebels. Nominations of tehsildars and provincial civil-service officers often threatened to act as wedges in the party's ranks, but Sir Sikandar had the good humour to postpone the publication of names till the Provincial Assembly session was over, so as to gain time until the next session. The rule of the bureaucracy, somewhat diluted by political nepotism, continued. Critical observers, mostly from the dispossessed non-agriculturist Hindu middle class, deplored the declining efficiency of the administration and the decided Muslim weightage in nepotism. Yet the Punjab was at peace, and visibly prosperous. The administration did not interfere too much with the daily life of the people: when the ministers are intent on personal ends, public affairs are mostly let alone. It is easier for a people to survive an indifferent government than a perverse one. The Punjab muddled along and might well have muddled through. The Unionists, united in self-interest, had unwittingly served public interest by providing a balance between the communities and letting sleeping (communal) dogs lie. The Congress-Unionist-Akali coalition of 1946 was a continuation of the old Unionist regime; it was merely a coalition against the Muslim League, held together by the opportunism of Unionist Muslims and the fear of Pakistan among Hindus and Sikhs. Some of the ministers of this coalition government were perhaps even more venal and less respected than their Unionist predecessors. The Principal of a college is reported to have said that the peon of the minister had a greater say in the appointments of his staff than he had. It was thus by no means a glorious regime. Later events were to show why such a government was tolerated for so long; it was a signpost, however faint, of the communal balance in the Punjab, the expression of a truth, however crude, which every Punjabi should have known, that no single community could rule the Punjab except at the expense of its peace and prosperity. Sir Sikandar and Sir Khizr played roles which were negative rather than positive; in the last stage, their regime was an insurance against communal anarchy, even though the premium in terms of inefficiency and nepotism may have been heavy.

Chapter II

The League Agitation

Early in February 1947 I happened to visit Jullundur for a day. Near the District Courts, I witnessed a procession of schoolboys. There was one slogan which arose above others: *Eent se eent baja denge, le ke rahenge Pakistan,* which may be translated as: 'We will achieve Pakistan, even if we have to blow up the whole continent.' These boys were repeating a slogan which reminded me of Rauschnigg's quotation from Hitler: 'Before I go down, I will leave the world in flames.' The innocent schoolchildren, the eldest of whom was in his teens, had only echoed a slogan heard from their teachers and parents. There were other slogans which mostly related to the various permutations and combinations in the Punjabi invective for Sir Khizr and his family. In the Congress Civil Disobedience campaigns there had been instances of such suffixes and prefixes as 'Hai, hai' or 'Down with' being attached to the names of various enemies of freedom, but these words would be the quintessence of politeness compared with the encyclopædia of vulgarity of which Sir Khizr became a target. Sensitive people, and some Congressmen, will always say: 'But this is wrong. Political battles cannot be won like this. This is not politics.' Muslim League leaders, however, have had no such ethical compunctions. Perhaps they argue that every thing is fair in hate and war. If it is within the laws of war to blast cities and blow up ships, why should it be wrong to blow opponents over with gusts of abuse? Hitler proved long ago that abuse of particular individuals (such as 'bloody-hound Benes,' or 'war-monger Churchill') or of particular communities such as the Jews, is the quickest means of rallying a docile following and of working up its emotions so as to silence opponents within and confuse opponents abroad. And it so happened that the Coalition Premier, Sir Khizr Hyat, was abused out of office.

The Muslim League represented its agitation as a campaign for civic rights for all Punjabis, and for the repeal of repressive laws. These professions were belied by the way the agitation started, by the refusal of the League leaders to allow police searches of their offices for arms; and the 'repressive laws' were the provisions of the Public Safety Ordinance which had kept the Province free from disorder when some other provinces had been torn by bloody strife. It appears in retrospect that the League, impatient for seizure of power in the Punjab, was only waiting for an opportunity. The banning of private armies like the Muslim League National Guards and the Rashtriya Swayam Sevak Sangh provided an opportunity. Those who consider this long overdue step on the part of the Khizr Ministry a blunder are confusing the occasion for the cause: the League would have precipitated matters anyhow. Its policies were dictated from above, from Aurangzeb Road, Delhi, where astute people were planning their next manoeuvre in close contact with British civilian advisers, whose attitude towards India was forty years behind the policy of the British Cabinet.

Chapter III

The Fatal Phrase

If I were asked who was immediately responsible for the Punjab disturbances in March 1946, I would name Mr. Attlee. This may sound a fantastic charge against the Premier 'who redeemed the British pledges to India.' The situation in the Punjab was, however, dramatically altered by the 20th February Statement in the House of Commons in which a date was named for the transfer of power to a Central Government or to existing provinces. It was the fate of almost all British declarations of policy on India that they became the subject of *post-mortem* by suspicious lawyers looking for weak points in the rival's case. The broad sweep, the abounding generosity, the great challenge inherent in the Statement of 20th February at once struck Pandit Nehru, who characterized it as 'a wise and courageous decision', and asked his fellow countrymen of all parties to cast off suspicion and fear. Muslim League leaders, however, lingered over one phrase which envisaged 'the transfer of power on due date whether as a whole to some form of Central Government for British India or in *some areas to the existing provincial governments. ...*' This phrase was a magic wand to them; it brought them nearer Pakistan than they had ever felt in their waking hours. The fixation of a final date for British withdrawal was a desperate and drastic remedy proposed by the British Cabinet; it made agreement not easier, but impossible. The League leaders thought that they had only to persevere in disagreement, and to keep out of the Constituent Assembly until June 1948 when Pakistan like a ripe mango would fall into their lap. The short period which spanned February 1947 and June 1948 did not strike them, as it struck the Congress leaders, as a challenge for forging a workable solution, but as a breathing space in which to capture and consolidate power in all provinces painted green in their minds. The Punjab, the N. W. F. P. and the Assam ministries became outposts which had to be captured before June 1948. 'Civil Disobedience movements' or 'direct-action movements' were launched or were intensified with unwonted vigour. In the N. W. F. P., by loot, murder and arson, the small prosperous minority was sought to be driven out and an attempt made to submerge political loyalties under communal frenzy. The Hazara district bordering on the Punjab, and more Punjabi than Pathan in population, set new standards in brutal fanaticism.

In the Punjab, the Muslim League movement remained surprisingly peaceful. Much was made of this later on, but there is no doubt that no Muslim League agitation had been less marked by bloodshed. There were several reasons for this immunity. The majority of Muslims had a genuine contempt for Sir Khizr's group and the movement was narrowed to a vituperative attack on 'Quisling Muslims'. The Hindus and Sikhs were told that they were spectators of a family quarrel of the Muslim community. There was no reaction from the minorities to some quite provocative demonstrations of the Leaguers. The provincial Government never really fought the movement: some Muslim officers and the police set the first bad example of conniving at open defiance of authority. If it was the decision of the Ministry to avoid repression, it had to thank itself for becoming the laughing stock of the world in the first week of the agitation; the spinelessness of the Khizr Ministry in February 1946 bears an instructive contrast to the firmness of the Pant Ministry in dealing with the Hindu Mahasabha agitation in the United Provinces in August 1947. Be it as it may, the Khizr Ministry contributed to its own downfall. The spell of the Public Safety Ordinance, which had held back turbulent elements in the Punjab, was broken. The police and the magistracy were demoralized; while token arrests went on, talks for a settlement were in progress between the League leaders and the Governor. Jail going was more a sport than a sacrifice when jail gates were expected to open any moment.

Those who tried to guess the upshot of the struggle by reviewing the number of processions and arrests could have more usefully riveted their eyes on Sir Khizr Hyat Khan. At the end of February he was easily the most hated Muslim in the Punjab. A perfect gentleman, with an old-world aristocratic courtesy, with undoubted personal integrity, with no pretensions to brilliance, he had strayed into politics like an English squire of the eighteenth century; he was devoid of personal or political passions and therefore lacked the courage of convictions. He did not perhaps realize that he was unwittingly the bastion of peace in the province. His presence gave to the minorities an assurance, perhaps a delusive one, against communal rule which the League victory in the last elections to the provincial legislature had brought perilously near. Sir Khizr Hyat, as I have remarked earlier, was abused out of office, but the abuse of the populace had been supplemented with the persuasions of politicians. It was impressed by Muslim League leaders on Sir Khizr that in view of the 20th February Statement a Muslim League ministry was essential to annex the Punjab to Pakistan by June 1948. Sir Mohammad Zafarullah was seen at Sir Khizr's residence in those fateful days and the visit was not merely a courtesy call. Later, Sir Khizr himself in a statement to the press made a cryptic reference to the changed situation in the Punjab after Mr. Attlee's statement. From the purely personal point of view Sir Khizr secured in the eyes of the Muslim League following a somewhat honourable exit from an unpopular position. From the political point of view, his resignation opened the sluice gates of anarchy.

Chapter IV

The March Riots

It is usual to link the March riots in the Punjab in the vicious chain, Calcutta, Noakhali, Bihar. Insofar as they witnessed gross brutality of the precedents set by the previous carnages, these riots were of the same order, but they were probably not a direct retaliation of the Muslims of the West Punjab to avenge the Bihar riots. Since August 1946, there has been a great moral recession in this country, and when people are angry they can exhibit levels of conduct to which they would not have stooped before. Any analysis of the Punjab riots which did not include a proper appreciation of the local and provincial factors would be superficial.

The March riots followed the downfall of the Khizr Ministry and the failure of the Muslim League to form a Ministry in the Punjab. The Muslim leaders and press affected amazement at the opposition of non-Muslim parties to the formation of the League Ministry. In the short lucid interval before the riots broke out, sweet words were spoken and written to tone down the non-Muslim opposition to a League Ministry. It was explained that a League Ministry in itself would not prejudge the issue in favour of Pakistan; but these assurances did not become those who had consistently opposed a national government at the Centre on the plea that it would prejudice the establishment of Pakistan. The political landscape had moreover been greatly altered by the 20th February Statement of Mr. Attlee; Sir Khizr had abdicated to let the League onto the throne to qualify for Pakistan in June 1948. Purely Muslim League ministries had been established in Sind and Bengal by means more foul than fair, and the reaction of Hindus and Sikhs was only one of passive, sullen discontent. The opposition of Hindus and Sikhs to a League Ministry in the Punjab may have been untenable on constitutional grounds; it was emotional in nature, though it sprang from the sense of self-preservation—from the fear that the League Ministry was a stepping stone to the establishment of Pakistan in June 1948.

The Muslim intelligentsia was convinced at the time by the press and politicians that the Sikhs were gratuitously provocative to the Muslims. There are various versions of the Sikh leaders' speeches; slogans of *Pakistan Murdabad* were alleged to have been raised and naked swords rattled in public. There is no doubt that many Sikh leaders have shown no sense of publicity; their utterances have been lacking in restraint and at least some of these utterances have been capable of being exploited by opponents to show them up as aggressors. The League leaders have themselves excelled in provocative speeches of which a brilliant example was the Muslim legislators' convention in Delhi at the time of the Cabinet Mission's visit. If *Pakistan Murdabad* was provocative to the Muslims of the Punjab in March, the slogan *Leke rahenge Pakistan, Jaise lia tha Hindustan* (We will achieve Pakistan in the same way in which we once conquered India) in February, was equally provocative to the Hindus and Sikhs; but Hindus and Sikhs had not been provoked by slogans to shed blood.

It is not my intention to reserve the monopoly of guilt to one party or another. It is, however, a useful habit to be introspective and self-critical; this is something for which Muslim League politicians and press have shown little capacity. By giving currency to specious pleas and extenuating arguments they have often prevented the full magnitude of the guilt coming home to the wrong-doers; on the other hand, they have helped the baser elements to rationalize their conduct in political terms. There was one statement which was repeated *ad nauseam* by the Muslim intelligentsia, that the Muslim Leaguers who were anxious to form a Ministry were in no mood to encourage riots, and that the boot was in fact on the other leg. The worst affected areas, however, were Rawalpindi and Multan Divisions, where the Hindus and Sikhs were too few to have taken the offensive, and even to have provided provocation. Almost the entire (present) East Punjab with the exception of

Gurgaon district remained quiet in March. In Lahore and Amritsar, the battle swayed this side and that; each community was alternately the aggressor and defender though the business and property of Hindus and Sikhs suffered most.

The March disturbances in the Western Punjab were widespread and the local causes in the districts and villages varied; very often, the occasion was a fancied grievance, a false rumour, an unwelcome slogan, a petty brawl. There was of course communal fanaticism (and the *Pirs* in these two Divisions are even now a force to reckon with) but there was also a considerable admixture of the purely predatory element. Some raiding parties brought camels, donkeys and carts to carry off the booty. Inevitably, old personal scores were paid off in a few cases, but as a rule the raid on the minority of a village was not made by the majority community of the same village, but of a different village. This is a very important point: the communal riots did not suddenly destroy the bonds of neighbourliness between immediate neighbours who could never commit such bestialities on each other as were perpetrated by outsiders. It was not an individual Muslim warring against an individual Sikh, but an individual Muslim at war with the Sikh community. This offers a parallel with the common attitude in international wars; an Englishman was waging war against the Germans, not against an individual German. The rules of organized international wars are of course different, but the parallel has been cited to drive home the truth that there were few cases in which the majority community in the same village attacked the minority living among them.

That there was some sort of organization behind the riots may be safely presumed. There were ex-soldiers, and 'demobbed' officers of 'martial traditions' many of whom had probably browsed through hot stuff served in some of the communal news sheets. In the districts of the Western Punjab it was not uncommon for a false alarm to be raised in the villages that a Sikh band (*Jatha*) was around the corner; and this alarm signal was doubly useful in collecting women and children in one place and in forming the male adults into a party for raiding villages in the vicinity.

When the riots broke out, and for weeks later, it was pointed out by some people that the riots occurred mostly in the districts, the Deputy Commissioners of which were Europeans. Pandit Jawaharlal Nehru and Sardar Patel hinted at the partiality of some of these officers. It would be unfair, however, to make a generalization. There were certainly some British officers who had an incurable habit of playing off communities against one another: the imminent termination of their careers after Mr. Attlee's statement of 20th February induced either frustration or indifference in them and it is not unlikely that they acted too late (and even then not strongly enough) in curbing the violence. Such officers, as could be said to have acted wilfully against preservation of peace, were, however, relatively few. The average British officer has a certain minimum amount of integrity for which he must not be denied credit. If the riots occurred in towns where British Deputy Commissioners were posted, it may be remembered that these districts were traditionally difficult from the communal point of view, and Britons had been selected to prevent the balance tilting in favour of one or the other community. The British officer, however, in dealing with large-scale communal disturbances had certain disadvantages; he had no such influence as his Indian counterpart could have in a district with a majority of Muslim population; a Muslim Deputy Commissioner in a period of acute communal tension could wield much influence with his own community in favour of restraint in the town; a Hindu Deputy Commissioner in the same district could not only keep up the morale of the minority community, but also use or may have been expected to use sufficient force in case of trouble. An Indian officer was also comparatively better informed: he could know the currents and cross-currents of public opinion; he could cajole, coax, coerce. The British officer, not knowing the language of the people, was dependent for news on his 'bearers' and 'peons', and inspectors of police who generally were small men with small minds. It was the police who in many cases misguided the British Deputy Commissioners and disabled them for effective action when the riots broke out. The British Raj had depended in the past on the prestige of the white man and on the docility, or at least the discipline, of the civil and police organizations. By March 1947, the prestige of the white face was at a low ebb; and the civil and police officials had been corrupted by communalism. Hence the ineffectiveness of the British district officers and the false position in which they often found themselves.

The March riots were quelled within 10 or 15 days by prompt and effective military action in Multan and Rawalpindi Divisions. The police were sneakingly communal, but the military, being composed of several communities and officered by Britons, Muslims, Hindus and Sikhs, could not openly take sides and the hooligan element could not have free play. It was significant that Mr. Jinnah did not visit areas where his followers had re-enacted the Noakhali, Calcutta and Bihar tragedies. If he had driven home to his followers unqualified disapproval of such aggression, and not contented himself with issuing belated and double-edged statements from Delhi, the West Punjab may not have lapsed into anarchy in August. Uncharitable critics have suggested that the shrewd, cold, calculating lawyer-leader considered these riots only another argument in his brief for the two-nation theory and the division of India. There is no doubt that the March riots finally broke the resistance of the Congress to the division of the country. Acharya Kripalani, the Congress President, observed later that the Congress was not afraid of the riots, but of the competitive degradation of communal frenzy which led to a continual lowering of individual morality and social conscience. Such sentiments were too metaphysical for the leaders of the Muslim League who saw the prize of Pakistan within their grasp. The riots, by reconciling the Congress to the partition of India, made Pakistan a practical proposition. They also made the partition of the Punjab a certainty.

Chapter V

The Lull between the Storms

From the end of March 1947 to the middle of August 1947 the western districts of the Punjab were comparatively quiet; but it was the silence of the grave. The military had been given extraordinary powers for dealing with the rioters, and the Central Government by energetic military action assisted the Governor of the Punjab, who ruled without a ministry, in restoring order in the affected districts; the army, the traditions of which had not yet been subjected to a 'sorting-out' of personnel on communal lines, proved an efficient instrument. The police had a questionable record in the affected districts and allegations of connivance at and even active assistance to the forces of disorder had been brought against it; the mixed composition of the police, however, made continued or open partiality impossible; police intervention in riots was yet a sort of sneaking affair.

Rawalpindi and Multan Divisions were quiescent by the beginning of April. These districts, however, did not return to normal in the true sense. Though refugee camps were opened, and there was talk of rehabilitating refugees, the minorities continued to migrate from villages to towns and from towns to other provinces and states. The feeling of security in its geographical aspect was relative; the villagers felt safer in their co-religionists' pockets in the towns, the town-dwellers from a fear of a repetition of the riots of March sought refuge in Hardwar, Dehru Dun, or Patiala.

The first two cities of the province, Lahore and Amritsar, which in March had not passed through the same horrors as the western districts, remained tense throughout the period from April to August. In both these cities communal warfare involved a series of ding-dong battles. The communities armed themselves for defence and offence in their strongholds and prepared for a battle of barricades which seemed inevitable to them. Communal armies gathered more recruits, more arms and more support from a public which had lost confidence in the forces of law and order. It was a preparation for a strange civil war, in which the population had no choice. It was not the kind of civil war at which the 'Cavaliers' and the 'Roundheads' had played in the seventeenth-century England; it was not the kind of civil war in which the Republicans and the Falangists ground each other in the twentieth-century Spain: one was not attacked for holding a different opinion from one's opponent, one was attacked for the crime of having been born to a father with a particular name and faith. Such was the excitement and suspicion into which the population of these towns had whipped themselves that money flowed from men of good positions and ample means for collecting swords, spears, guns, petrol and jeeps. There is a peculiar tendency on the part of guns to go off by themselves if they have accumulated beyond a certain number; in the international as well as in national affairs, the surest way of precipitating a conflict is to arm for self-defence; and after all, as somebody said, 'Offence is the best form of defence.'

There was one ominous aspect of the communal tension of this period, particularly after the partition of the Punjab became a certainty, in that some executive officers, whose function was to keep the peace between the communities, vied with one another in establishing a 'reputation' for being loyal crusaders of their community; to careerists such a 'reputation' was an 'investment' for the future, but this private ambition shattered public morale. When the *Shahalmi* area of Lahore was burnt down during curfew hours under the very nose of the police and presumably with their connivance, it was a turning point in the communal warfare. Such a large number of Hindus and Sikhs left Lahore after this incident that a friend wrote to me from Lahore in early August that if the Boundary Commission awarded Lahore to non-Muslims, they would have to 're-conquer' it from Muslims. Those custodians of law and order who failed to do their duty to the residents of *Shahalmi* locality set a bad example for the disturbances in the two Punjabs in the middle of August which drove millions of men, women and children of all communities from their homes in a panicky flight for life to the frontier.

In general the morale of the public between the riots of March and the anarchy of August vibrated to the tune of high politics. It was at a low ebb when Lord Wavell left; there was almost a shameful rise in public confidence when Lord Mountbatten appeared on the scene something like a *deus ex mahina;* there was a sudden drop on the eve of Lord Mountbatten's announcement regarding the transfer of power when people argued that it was as impossible to produce a solution which would suit both the parties as to make two parallel lines meet. The tension in the Punjab at the end of May and in the beginning of June was so acute that most people kept a night vigil on housetops, or slept with their hands on the trigger of the pistol under the pillow. Lord Mountbatten sensed this tension; not only did he increase military precautions in the tense district, but he arranged simultaneously with his announcement for broadcasts from Pandit Jawaharlal Nehru, Mr. M.A. Jinnah and Sardar Baldev Singh, all of whom appealed for peace. Pandit Jawaharlal Nehru directly committed himself and indirectly the Indian National Congress to the acceptance of Lord Mountbatten's plan; Sardar Baldev Singh almost rashly ratified the plan (with all its faults) on behalf of the Sikh community; even Mr. Jinnah, for once, took the public into his confidence by revealing his personal reactions and the feeling in Delhi Muslim League circles—though with his inborn democratic instinct, and as the constitutional president of the Muslim League, he could not commit his party without the mandatory advice of its Council. Anyhow the public on hearing the broadcasts of the Viceroy and the three great leaders on the same evening heaved a sigh of relief. But broadcasts, however assuring, could not magically purge the smouldering hatreds and consuming fears which had accumulated for months; these emotions could only go underground and it is not surprising that they came up again at the first provocation.

Chapter VI

August Disturbances

In all quarrels, from a street brawl to a global war, it is usual for each side to tell the other, 'You started it'. In September 1939, the majority of the Germans believed, or rather were made to believe, that Poland, egged on by Britain and France, had invaded German soil. Less than two years later, as the *blitz* against Russia commenced, the story was put out from the German radio and press that Hitler had merely forestalled a Soviet offensive against Germany. Even Mussolini, to the amusement of many foreigners, described his invasion of Albania and Greece as a 'defensive measure'. In China, the Communists and Kuomintang simultaneously blame each other for taking the offensive. This debate as to who fired the first shot is, from a practical point of view, a mere waste of breath. There are more promising lines of investigation. Why was the first shot not the last?

Why did it begin an unending echo of explosions and counter-explosions?

Cataclysmic conflicts are almost invariably preceded and to some extent precipitated by a general sense of high tension. As I write this, I recall a passage in Sir Nevile Henderson's book *The Failure of A Mission,* in which he describes how before the actual outbreak of the war, Goering at a private dinner, on hearing a loud explosion, exclaimed: 'The damned British have started it,' and how to the subsequent discomfiture of the Field Marshal and to the amusement of the British Ambassador, it was discovered that the explosion was due to the dynamiting of a derelict building in the neighbourhood.

A similar tension had prevailed in the Punjab during the six months preceding the partition. The origins of this tension and its ebb and flow have been traced in the preceding chapters. Throughout this period, some districts of the Punjab were in the throes of a virtual civil war; the others had the dubious consolation of an armed peace. June 3, 1947, the date on which Britain's final plan for transfer of power to India was to be announced by the last Viceroy bade fair to become the 'D Day' for the launching of anarchy in the Punjab. Lord Mountbatten's diplomatic skill and military precautions, however, seemed to have averted the catastrophe by a hair's breadth.

The 'June 3 Plan' broke the deadlock which had gripped Indian politics for nearly eight years. Its acceptance by the principal parties was an event which, in the light of recent failures, seemed too good to be true. Mr. Attlee's cabinet had cause for satisfaction at the triumphant conclusion to which its Indian policy had drifted. The Indian National Congress was visibly relieved at the near prospect of the final and the formal end of foreign rule in India. The All India Muslim League was jubilant at the attainment of its cherished goal of Pakistan. There was a new and cheerful note in Indian politics, which generated the hope that leaders of Britain, the Indian National Congress and the Muslim League would bury the hatchet and part as friends. The Partition Council composed of the representatives of both the future dominions issued from Delhi a series of communiques which promised a peaceful partition of the country. This new-born cordiality among the political leaders after years of acrimonious controversy was heartening, but it did not percolate to the lower levels where public opinion was—and continues to be—moulded, not by official communiques but by petty pensioners or the rabid vernacular press. Mr. Jinnah had, to use an Americanism, 'sold' his Pakistan to the Muslim masses as a blueprint for an Islamic State. The secular qualities of the article may have always been in his mind but he advertised them a little too late to ensure before the appointed date of 15th August the conversion of the Muslim League rank and file and the confidence of the non-Muslim minorities.

Lord Mountbatten's plan, which steadied Indian politics by compelling the politicians to get down to brass tacks, contained in its execution the seeds of a conflict. The plan outlined a partition of the assets and liabilities of the British government of India between the two successor states. The homely analogy for this process, which, incidentally, was often cited in the interminable debate on Pakistan, is the division of property in an Indian joint family. It is well known that, while the decision to separate clears the air and restores something of the almost forgotten cordiality among brothers and their wives, the actual division of the property is accompanied by a fresh crescendo of bitter recrimination. Peace is, however, preserved by the tears of the bewildered father (if he has the misfortune to be alive), or by the intercession of disinterested neighbours—or in the last resort by the police and the courts. The process of the partition of the Indian administration resembled the typical story of a joint family; the politicians who had welcomed the announcement of partition, when actually brought face to face in the Partition Council, wrangled bitterly over the distribution of almost everything from uncovered debts to inkpots. There were more parting kicks than kisses but, unfortunately, there were no such arbiters for dividing the administration as are available to a joint family; the latter may call in the police and the courts, but what could these guardians of law and order do if they themselves were the subjects of division? The British Government had no intention to play the role of a disinterested neighbour, much less of a father; Sir Stafford Cripps, conscious of the manpower shortage in industry, had no British boys to send to India and

Mr. Bevin was already breaking his shins against the terrorists in Palestine. Moreover, it is an interesting fact that though in the midst of a war allies pool divisions and even armies for the occupation of 'strategic' areas, they would not collect even a few regiments in peace time for the thankless job of an international police. The U.N.O., while sanctioning the partition of Palestine, has discreetly omitted the setting up of a neutral police force strong enough for enforcing its division.

The process of partition in the Punjab (and Bengal) involved the reshuffling of personnel on communal lines in all ranks of the administration. The set-up in the Punjab had already been weakened by ten years of 'Provincial Autonomy'. Among the civil servants, there were many who had owed their professional fortunes to political favours: in the days of the Unionist rule, they were bastions of vested interests against popular movements, and when that regime was crumbling, they became the pillars of the movement for Pakistan, which seemed to them a paradise for quick promotions. Communalism had set in more in the Provincial services than in the Central services, and more among the Subordinate-service officials than in the Provincial services. The Punjab Police had never been popular but it had a reputation for 'toughness'; its Muslim majority had made it suspect to Hindus and Sikhs since the riots in the western districts in March 1947, but so long as the police force, and for that matter, the general administration was jointly manned by Hindus, Muslims,

Sikhs and Britons it could not become universally or brazenly communal.

The immediate risks inherent in the reconstruction of an administration which was notorious neither for its honesty nor for political neutrality were increased by the provisional or 'notional' division of the province. The very idea of a notional division impeded the timely crystallization of public attitudes which was necessary for the new set-up; it prolonged the period of vague expectancy among the people. Yet it was inherent in the nature of the 'June 3 Plan' and inevitable in the prevalent mood of the politicians. Lord Mountbatten's plan for the partition of India prescribed a procedure for democratic decisions by elected representatives of the people; but what with the details of the procedure and what with the policies of the political parties, these decisions were foregone conclusions. Lord Mountbatten will go down in history as a great 'sailor-salesman'. The success of a salesman lies not only in offering good wares but in making the customers believe that the wares are 'just the thing' they want. Lord Mountbatten went so far as to say that the constitutional plan was made not by himself but by the Indian political leaders themselves. If he had been less careful than he was, he may have included a 'boundary award' in his plan. In parenthesis it may be noted that the political parties in the past refused to concede to one another what they subsequently surrendered under British awards, without of course ceasing to cast aspersions on the honesty of the British broker. In 1947, the British broker was winding up his business in India and was keen in this last phase not to do anything which might affect the goodwill he was leaving behind. Lord Mountbatten, therefore, took particular care to dissociate himself from the responsibility for the demarcation of the frontiers between India and Pakistan; he lifted this contentious subject from the political plane to a judicial pedestal by securing the agreement of the parties to the setting up of a Boundary Commission composed of High Court judges and presided over by Sir Cyril Radcliffe, an eminent British lawyer. Once the matter rested with the lawyers and judges it was bound to take time and meanwhile the deadline of 15th August drew near. The Punjab had been without a ministry since the beginning of March. The Governor, Sir Evans Jenkins, who had been sitting on the fence all the time, had been pelted with stones from both sides; he had some idea of the temper of the people and he may have heard of the grim boast of Mr. Suhrawardy, the Muslim League Premier of Bengal, that his government, which was in occupation of Calcutta, would not surrender it to the Hindus in the event of partition of Bengal, without reducing the great city to something like a shambles. On the eve of the partition, Muslims, Hindus and Sikhs, arguing from different premises, seemed to agree that even the provisional possession of the entire province would be nine-tenths of the legal ownership. This explains why Muslims opposed the provisional or 'notional' division of the province as vehemently as the non-Muslims wanted it.

When mutual confidence was almost non-existent, a provisional partition was a short-term expedient to diminish the area and the occasions of conflict. In actual fact, just the opposite result was achieved. A provisional boundary line would have been a stabilizing factor if it had been declared, subject to only minor rectifications. The Radcliffe Commission was, however, untrammelled by any such limitation and it was free to draw a boundary line anywhere after hearing the claims of the parties. Of claims there was no end. Nearly half of the province was disputed between the two new states and these districts came to be styled, during the interim period, as 'Border Districts'. The imagination of the public and the press received a dangerous impetus. Statistics of land revenue, moveable and immovable property, income-tax, population, schools, colleges, firms, factories, temples, 'gurdwaras', and mosques were compiled by able lawyers and piled on the Boundary Commission. The editors of the vernacular newspapers appeared to believe that Sir Cyril Radcliffe would supplement the arguments of lawyers with editorials in the vernacular press. Political controversy and press propaganda reached a new pitch, whipping up public excitement at a time when restraint in language was the prime necessity. An attempt was made to mitigate the sense of insecurity in the districts, the final destiny of which depended upon the award of the Boundary Commission, by the formation of a Boundary Force composed of troops of both the future dominions. It appeared at the time that a joint force to police the disputed districts, during the critical days of the partition until the boundary award was implemented, would be a guarantee of peace. The Boundary Force was, in fact, only another strand in an intricate tangle; to appraise its part in preventing, putting down and, in some cases, perhaps, aggravating the disturbances, it is necessary to review the condition of the Indian army as it existed on the eve of the partition.

During World War II, Field Marshal Auchinleck had made some amends for the British mistrust of Indians since the Sepoy Mutiny of 1857, by broadening the field of recruitment to include non-martial races and by encouraging a spirit of *camaraderie* which the battlefields of North Africa, Europe and South-East Asia had further cemented. As the War drew to a close and the men returned home, the two-nation theory and the movement for a 'sovereign Pakistan,' in which the division of the army on communal lines was implicit, put the wartime *camaraderie* to a severe test. During the last phase of the political controversy on Pakistan, Malik Feroze Khan Noon said: 'He who has the army has India', but the bombshell was not so terrific as he had intended it to be. The Congress leader, Dr. Rajendra Prasad, declared that if the Muslim League insisted on a separate army, it could have it as part of the sovereign Pakistan. Mahatma Gandhi, however, referred to the dangers inherent in the creation of two armies out of one and the possibility of a ruinous armament race at the expense of the already impoverished common man. The *Statesman* published an editorial, the title of which,

'Armed Rabble', expressed the writer's fear of the anarchy which the division of the army would let loose on the land. The future rulers of Pakistan were, however, in no mood to surrender an essential attribute of sovereignty. At long last, the fateful directive came from the Partition Council for 'sorting out' the armed forces on communal lines; old bonds dissolved overnight; the links of comradeship snapped; the traditions and the discipline of the army received a sudden blow and the resultant psychological shock largely explains the conduct of certain troops in the communal disturbances—a conduct to which public reference has been made by responsible ministers of both India and Pakistan.

It was against this background that the Boundary Force was formed. It was a well-meaning move but good intentions and reasoned calculations were upset by human variables. The composite force had one General but not common loyalty. Major-General Rees's position in the Punjab was not even that of General Marshall in China. It has been alleged that the Boundary Force failed to act with sufficient cohesion, strength and impartiality. To some extent its lack of success was due to the fact that the disturbances exceeded the anticipated scale and area, but, even in the districts where it was stationed, its record was not in keeping with the traditions of the Indian Army. The exponents of a world state include in their plans an international police force for use against recalcitrant states, but an international police force is of no use unless its members have a super-national loyalty. The experience of the Punjab is a portent of no small significance. The Punjab Boundary Force was not drawn from the armies of two independent countries; it was a part of the great Indian Army, which was being split into two separate units. There was no question of forging new links and developing a new loyalty in a composite force; it was merely a question of old loyalties lasting for another month or so. The dissolution of the Boundary Force organization was accompanied by the usual military ceremonial which deceived nobody. There was a distinct improvement from the date the two governments assumed direct responsibility within their respective dominions.

The sorting out of the civil administration and the army was a *sine qua non* for the establishment of Pakistan. To build new cadres and to make them function required time; an administrative vacuum, though it was possible to reduce its duration, was inevitable. The continuity implicit in the adage 'The King is dead, long live the King' is a royal prerogative and does not belong to the paraphernalia of his government. Attempts were made to prevent anarchy slipping into the temporary vacuum; these attempts failed in the Punjab and would have failed in Bengal if Mahatma Gandhi had not acted as a sentry. There was, however, a certain contradiction between communal peace and Pakistan; it was inherent in the goal of the Muslim League and in its method. The Muslim League's drastic remedy for the minority problem made the disease worse—if not incurable. There are two pillars on which the honourable existence of a minority in an independent state depends: the goodwill of the majority and a fair share in the running of the government and administration. The movement for Pakistan undermined the first pillar; the establishment of Pakistan knocked off the second. Mr. Jinnah told the Pakistan Constituent Assembly in August that Pakistan guaranteed equal rights and equal obligations for Muslims, Hindus, Sikhs and Christians. Yet in a province like the Punjab, where the communities were balanced not only numerically but also politically, a major guarantee of non-communal rule was the continuance of an administration in which all communities were represented. Yet, after 15th August 1947 the partitioned provinces and the two Central governments were left with a smaller residue of minority representation than ever before.

Mr. Jinnah had himself called upon Muslim government servants to follow him to Pakistan to build up 'the greatest Islamic State in the world'. Most of these men had been the spearheads of the Pakistan movement, and they responded to the Qaid-e-Azam's call. They also knew which side their bread was buttered; there were likely to be new jobs and quick promotions in a new State and above all there would be no Hindu colleagues who were such sticky competitors. A stampede occurred among the Hindu and Sikh officials in provinces which were to be formed into Pakistan; they opted for service in the Indian Dominion. The problem, therefore, was how to ensure non-communal rule in each of the two States which had increasingly to function through the members of only the majority community. Sardar Patel once said, 'Pakistan means civil war'. Dr. Syed Abdul Latif predicted in 1941 that 'Mr. Jinnah's politics will decidedly lead to civil war'. These warnings, though unpalatable to the Qaid-e-Azam at the time, were nevertheless prophetic. 'Direct action'—or to take the Muslim League leaders at their word, the threat of direct action to achieve Pakistan—caused more blood to be shed in internecine strife in one year than had been spilled in the previous half a century. But even that year's flow was a mere rivulet compared with the torrential river which flowed in the month following the establishment of Pakistan. So long as the country was united and the administration in varying degrees was a joint concern, communal disturbances, whether in Noakhali, Bihar, or the West Punjab, were localized and quelled in comparatively short periods. The disturbances in the East and the West Punjabs after the partition defied attempts at localization. That they were eventually quelled was a poor consolation to the minorities who continued to be routed across the border. The governments of the two Punjabs were finally faced with the grim fact that few Hindus and Sikhs could stay in the West Punjab and few Muslims in the East Punjab. The two Punjabs in their respective populations now reflect a homogeneity of communal composition which the partition had at first imparted to their administration.

Indeed, it is now no longer a mere question of the composition of the government or the personnel of the administration. Even if it were possible to restore the composite character of the government in the two Punjabs, it would still be impossible for the minorities to return to their homes. True rehabilitation, in the sense in which Mahatma Gandhi understands it, is no longer feasible. Communal passion is a passing emotion; the vested interest in property is more permanent. When the first wave of blind violence had passed in the West Punjab, the lure of loot was the chief motive for violence; calculated homicide succeeded indiscriminate violence; it was no longer a fanatic's leap in the dark but an adventurer's firm foothold on a house, a shop, or a factory. A leading article on 'Corruption' in the British-owned *Civil & Military Gazette* of Lahore, in its issue of the 20th November, 1947, referred to 'the occasions created by the minority evacuation for the personal aggrandizement in the shape of frankly criminal looting or more respectable but equally criminal 'protective custody' without authorization. People in every rank of life, from the highest to the lowest, found it impossible to resist the chance of a rich harvest while the sun of disorder shone'. In his book, *An Australian in India,* Mr. Casey, the ex-Governor of Bengal, writes:

In other words I believe that the principal present-day motive behind Pakistan is the economic urge on the part of the Muslims (particularly in the cities) to advance themselves economically. ... I believe that when the Muslims in a village or a small town think of Pakistan, they think in terms of the little village or town store being owned, by a Muslim and not by a Hindu. When the city

Muslim thinks of Pakistan, I believe he thinks largely in terms of the mills and shops and business houses being owned by Muslims instead of by Hindus. ... But the fact remains that, Pakistan or no Pakistan, Hindus and Muslims have got to continue to live together. ... Pakistan would not result in the village store being owned by a Muslim. It would not put the mills and the business houses into Muslim hands. The only way Muslims can advance themselves economically is to achieve education, and to learn how to compete successfully with the Hindus, which means a vast amount of hard work and the passage of time. It cannot be achieved by political means.*

Mr. Casey has proved a false prophet; for in western Pakistan all the village and town stores and shops and factories which were owned by Hindus and Sikhs are in the hands of Muslims. Mr. Casey could not see the August anarchy, which brought about an economic revolution. A reverse position exists in the East Punjab; the complaint in fact is that the Muslim evacuees have not left enough lands, stores, shops, or factories for occupation by the refugees from the West Punjab. The vested interest in property is now a factor to be reckoned with; it is stronger in the West Punjab because the possessions of non-Muslim evacuees were greater than those of the Muslims in the East Punjab. There is no

---

* R. G. Casey, *An Australian in India,* pp. 76-77.

doubt that the 'August Revolution' in the Punjab rests now on the sure foundations of vested interests, which in the past buttressed such respectable movements as the English Reformation and the French Revolution.

Chapter VII

Anarchy Unchecked

I have tried to review in the preceding chapters the background of the August disturbances and their underlying causes. It is more difficult to describe the sequence of events and to assess the responsibility for the actual outbreak. The Prime Minister of Pakistan has alleged that there was a conspiracy in the Indian Dominion for the extermination of its Muslim minority. The latest revelation has come from the Governor-General of Pakistan himself; according to Mr. Jinnah, India had plotted the riots to pull out the Hindu and Sikh minorities in order to disrupt the economy of Pakistan—and incidentally to disrupt her own economy. So far from having planned the 'August Anarchy', the Indian leaders were taken entirely unawares by it. The trouble had already started before the 15th of August when the capital of India abandoned itself to the joyous celebrations of the dawn of freedom. In his Hindustani version of the speech in the Constituent Assembly in that historic midnight session of 15th August 1947, Pandit Jawaharlal Nehru interpolated a brief but poignant reference to 'the heat of the burning cities which are not far off'. But this plaintive note was drowned in the chorus of popular joy and excitement. Subsequent events provided cynics with the cheap gibe that Delhi was fiddling while the Punjab was burning and bleeding. That Gandhi, Nehru and Patel planned 'Operation Extermination' in the Punjab in August and that Gandhiji went to Calcutta and Nehru and Patel stayed at Delhi to create evidence of alibi—this should be too big a lump even for willing throats in Pakistan to swallow. The Congress leaders had seen enough of murder, loot and arson in the preceding year and it was to end the vicious cycle of violence that they had agreed to pay the price of partition. If the Congress leaders had really intended to pull out the minorities, their advice to Hindus and Sikhs to stay on in Pakistan could have only one fantastic explanation that they were throwing a smokescreen to deceive the Muslim League and that they considered evacuation of Hindu and Sikh minorities without personal and movable property at the expense of the Government of India superior to a 'bag and baggage' migration at private expense even of those people who desired to get out while the going was good. Allegations of a conspiracy are the stock-in-trade of totalitarian propaganda and do not now evoke even the smile they used to do when they were first trotted out by Fascist States. The spokesmen of the Government of

India have not made any countercharges of a conspiracy in Pakistan to drive out the non-Muslim minorities. Presumably the Intelligence Service of the Indian Dominion is not so efficient as that of Pakistan.

The theory of a conspiracy does not help in ascertaining the causes of the outbreak, nor can any useful purpose be served by assessing the comparative losses of the communities in life and property. In a province where a correct census of the living was difficult in comparatively peaceful times, any attempt at computation of the dead after a violent upheaval would only be a wild guess. Even if death rolls could be computed with any measure of accuracy, they could hardly throw any light on the causes of the disorders. A historian who sets out to assess the relative responsibility of Germany, Britain, Japan and America for precipitating World War II by comparing the destruction of Warsaw, London, Rotterdam, Cologne, Singapore and Hiroshima, or the death rolls of these nations, is engaged in a hopeless venture.

In the Punjab, incidents which inflamed the various towns and villages must have varied; but for the political and social context in which they occurred, they would not have caused the havoc they did. For example, it was known that in the second week of August, armed gangs were roaming the countryside in some districts of the East Punjab; how far their activities were inspired by communal and how far by predatory motives was a moot point. Some instances during this period did, however, savour of a belated retaliation by Sikh refugees from the West Punjab and their relatives and sympathisers in the East Punjab for the atrocities committed on the Sikh community in Rawalpindi and Multan Divisions in March 1947. In all probability, these sporadic acts of disorder would have been put down if the East Punjab Government had had time to get into the saddle. Unfortunately, a similar and simultaneous lawlessness existed in certain areas of the West Punjab. These sporadic incidents in themselves were neither unexpected nor very alarming. That some disorder might break out had been anticipated and provided against; what was not anticipated was the wildfire speed with which it spread, the area which it engulfed and its unwonted violence. It is difficult to say which was the first link and which was the last in a chain of tragic events in Amritsar, Lahore, Wazirabad, Sialkot, Ferozepore, Gujranwala, Jullundur and Sheikhupura. It was like the 'chain reaction of an atomic explosion'.

In the third week of August, the question posed by the rulers of Pakistan was 'Who started first?' The Indian leaders were, however, more concerned with the question 'Who will stop first?' On the morrow of the Independence Day celebrations, Pandit Jawaharlal Nehru threw himself heart and soul into the ordeal of the Punjab. He had already taken the precaution of appointing Sir Chandulal Trivedi, an experienced administrator, as the Governor of the East Punjab, who shifted his headquarters from Simla to Jullundur with an improvised secretariat. The Central Government helped the East Punjab Government in establishing in record time a network of communications, which dispensed with the grudging co-operation from Lahore. Troops were rushed to the scenes of trouble. The ministers of the Indian Government contacted their opposite numbers in Pakistan for a joint attack on the menace of lawlessness. To his own people, Pandit Nehru spoke in clear and unmistakable terms: that India was a secular democratic state, and that communal rioters, regardless of their religious labels, were traitors. Though the government probably knew the worst about the happenings in the West Punjab, it withheld the publication of blood-curdling accounts. The All India Radio in the first week or so after the outbreaks practised in its references to the West Punjab an extraordinary restraint; I know of at least one instance in which unsuspecting passengers from Central India, misled by the discreet or perhaps indiscreet silence of the All India Radio, and unaware of the disorders in the West Punjab, travelled by rail to Lahore and beyond—and have not been heard of since. By contrast, the Radio Pakistan drew an iron curtain on the events in the West Punjab but horrified its listeners with hair-raising accounts of the 'atrocities' in the East Punjab. The foreign correspondents, who were free to move about in the East Punjab, sent sensational stories to their papers; since the West Punjab was a sealed book to them, they lacked the knowledge, even if they had the will, for the juxtaposition of events on both sides of the border, which was essential for a true perspective and for grasping the deeper causes of the outbreak, the reasons for its intensity and its wide incidence. As it was, Pakistan secured a 'good press' abroad. A typical comment may be cited from the usually staid British journal, *The Economist,* dated the 30th August, 1947:

> It was expected that the worst trouble arising from the partition of India would come from Sikhs... the boundary award has in fact for economic reasons given less of the Punjab to Pakistan than the mere statistics of communal distribution would require but the fury of Sikhs has not been assuaged and has broken out in an organized campaign to exterminate or drive out all Muslims left on the Indian side of the border. ... By these actions, the Sikhs have exposed their co-religionists on the Pakistan side of the frontier to reprisals in kind.

Sir Mohd. Zafrullah Khan, leader of Pakistan's delegation to the United Nations General Assembly, levelled reckless charges against the Indian Government and started washing dirty linen before an international audience; the dirty linen was of course largely his own but he wanted to foist its ownership exclusively on the Indian Government. A public fed on 'atrocity stories' and a favourable foreign press, which had not yet had time for second thoughts, these were certainly feathers in the politician's cap, but by themselves they were powerless to stop a tidal wave of violence.

There is no doubt about this wave of violence which swept Pakistan in the very hour of its birth. The propagandist with an eye on the foreign press may ignore it or belittle it, but the administrators knew and also the victims. Sir Francis Mudie, the Governor of the West Punjab, is reported to have told a conference of the Deputy Commissioners of the province that 'when the present Government took over, Lahore was in flames and there was musketry fire going all round my house. Stories of appalling atrocities were coming in almost every hour and there seemed to be no end to them. It looked at one time that even the Army and the Police might fail us and everything would dissolve in chaos'. The Quaid-i-Azam and his followers could meet this crisis in one of two ways. One was the line of least resistance; it was less difficult for the leaders and more popular with the mob. The other was to condemn the violence unequivocally and to follow up abortive persuasion with ruthless suppression of recalcitrants irrespective of their past services. Unfortunately, the course of least resistance was preferred. One of the first acts of the West Punjab Government was to remove the restrictions on the possession of swords. Even as the conflagration had started, the Prime Minister of Pakistan reeled off from Karachi statement after statement on the 'atrocities' in the East Punjab and their likely 'repercussions' on the Muslim majority in Pakistan whose patience was 'sorely tried'.

The Father of the Pakistan nation and the Head of the Pakistan State, Quaid-i-Azam Mohd. Ali Jinnah, might have stopped the rot if he had acted promptly and vigorously. Apparently his health did not permit him to visit Lahore until it was too late and then too he, as the Governor-General, had so much on his hands that he had to disappoint deputations of the public which had applied for interviews.

Mahatma Gandhi, slightly older than the Quaid-i-Azam, was, however, blessed with better health and was strong enough to roam the streets of Calcutta preaching the brotherhood of man from door to door. Hindus and Muslims fraternized on 15th August in common celebration of the newly-found freedom. People called it a miracle wrought by Mahatma Gandhi. Actually, it was no miracle; it was not a magician's trick but the hard-won victory of a brave fighter against heavy odds. Exactly a year ago, on 16th August 1946—the Muslim League's Direct Action Day—communal violence had been unleashed upon Calcutta and had like a mighty river in spate continued to engulf more and more cities, villages and provinces of the fair land of India. To this violence Gandhiji had reacted with deep anguish of body, mind and spirit and he had no weapons except of *Ahimsa* or non-violence with which he could fight the evil. Such was the terrific force of the violence that many, even among his followers, began to think that his creed, though a successful patent for the foreigners, could not work on the Indian constitution and in any case its curative action appeared to be imperceptibly slow. Even Gandhiji, as he limped on blistered feet in the paddy-fields of Noakhali, admitted that he was groping in darkness. When a Muslim villager asked him why there was neither Pakistan nor peace, Gandhiji had no answer.

On 15th August 1947, peace returned to Bengal but not through Pakistan, for in the very heart and soul of Pakistan, there raged a tornado of violence. Peace came to Bengal through the bowl of a beggar who begged from the citizens of riot-torn Calcutta for a little mutual forgiveness and goodwill. With mingled hope and misgiving, Gandhiji watched Calcutta's Hindus and Muslims locked in an embrace in the celebration of common freedom; was it the glow of communal harmony or merely the flush of excitement? A few days later, Hindus and Muslims, inflamed by the news from the Punjab, were again at each other's throat; they were separated not by the batons of the police, nor by the rifles of the military but by the sacrificial fast of one who had staked his life so that others might not die. Jinnah could have saved Lahore and the Punjab just as Gandhiji had saved Calcutta and Bengal. He, however, was no Gandhi; the only Muslim leader who could do the beggar's part was Khan Abdul Ghaffar Khan, the Frontier Gandhi. But Abdul Ghaffar Khan was Jinnah's *bete noire;* the N.W.F.P. Ministry headed by Ghaffar's brother, despite its majority in the legislature, was marking time for a death warrant from the Governor-General of Pakistan.

It must, however, be conceded that the failure of the leaders of Pakistan to act decisively on the first impact of the crisis was partly due to the peculiar disadvantages from which they suffered. The crisis called for a cool head and a heavy hand. A fair proportion of the personnel of the Pakistan Central Cabinet and Secretariat were, however, drawn from provinces which were either disturbed or highly tense. The Indian Cabinet, the majority of whose members were drawn from unaffected provinces, could more easily take a detached and long-term view; without ceasing to be responsive to public opinion it could rise above popular passions. The editorial of the *Civil & Military Gazette* from which I have already quoted referred to the 'rising tide of governmental impotence and public frustration,' and nearly two months earlier this newspaper had bluntly told the West Punjab Government 'to govern or get out'. The primary cause of government impotence had been the Muslim League National Guards organization. It was founded as a counterblast to the Congress Seva Dals (Volunteer Corps). The Congress Volunteer Corps had, however, a long tradition of service and sacrifice; they had been generally organized under the control of the local Congress Committees. They had been trained to control, with folded hands, crowds in processions and meetings, or to picket liquor shops. From the outset they had been bound—so far as any large organization can be bound—by the non-violent creed of the Congress. The background of the National Guards of the Muslim League has, however, been very different from that of the Congress Seva Dal. The growth of the National Guards coincided with the hectic year of 1946 and the threat of the Muslim League's 'Direct Action'. In the Punjab the local Muslim Leagues had been able to exercise either a nominal authority or none at all over local 'Salars' (leaders) of the National Guards. The National Guards have a pyramidal organization; implicit obedience to the immediate superior is a duty of every member and there is a whole hierarchy of 'Salars'. There have been no irksome restraints on this organization regarding means *versus* ends, violence *versus* non-violence, and its members as the vanguard of the Pakistan Revolution have worn helmets and driven in jeeps; but they have never known police batons, which left lasting scars on the bare backs of Congress volunteers in former times. During the August disturbances in the West Punjab, the National Guards played a special role in the pursuit of the minorities. While the Prime Minister of Pakistan pledged peace and protection to the minorities and entered into commitments with the Indian Dominion regarding the protection and evacuation of the non-Muslim minorities and the West Punjab Government issued neat communiques on these subjects, the local 'Salars' of the Muslim National Guards with the friendly co-operation of the sub-inspectors of police and local hooligans pursued an independent course. Against this background, it would seem that the Government of India's protests about 'breach of promise' regarding evacuation arrangements did not make full allowance for the internal pressures in Pakistan.

Once again, faced with a critical challenge, the leaders of Pakistan chose the line of least resistance; instead of attempting to scotch the Frankenstein monster of a private army, they conferred on it the reassuring title of 'Home Guards', legalized its *de facto* possession of arms and proclaimed its intention to give proper military training to its members. There would be nothing new or surprising about the raising of a 'Home Guard' such as was raised in Great Britain in the dark days of 1940. To raise a 'Home Guard' *de novo* from the civilian population for a limited period is something very different from the official recognition of a private army which had a past record of a doubtful nature. The line of least resistance may mean eventually the greater resistance; short-term expedients are often the foundations of a long-term disaster. Pakistan's private army may soon be its own problem, if indeed it has not already become one. A private army which is the ally of a political party today may become its master tomorrow. So long as it suits it, a private army like the S.S. troops of the Nazi party may follow in the train of a dominant political leader or his party, but at any stage it may swerve to a political career under an ambitious commander who may not go down as easily as Captain Roehm did in 1934. It may be argued that private armies have existed on both sides of the border; the attitude of the Indian Government offers, however, an instructive contrast to that of the Government of Pakistan. Neither the Government of India nor the Indian National Congress has recognized these bodies nor have they refrained from expressing their disapproval of the existence of any organization which impinges on the role of the police and the armed forces. Individual freedom and parliamentary democracy are entirely incompatible with the existence of a body of men who can be used for dragooning political opponents or racial or religious groups.

To return to the predicament of the leaders of

Pakistan. There is no denying the fact that their difficulties were greater than those of their neighbours, but their efforts were also less bold and less whole-hearted. It requires a great deal of courage to face up to public clamour. Criticism grates on ears used to homage so that in a crisis, a politician is often tempted to follow instead of guiding public opinion. Pandit Jawaharlal Nehru was one of the most unpopular men in Bihar in October 1946 when he threw his personal and official weight against the frenzy of his co-religionists; his unpopularity in Delhi among the West Punjab refugees and their sympathisers during the months of August and September 1947 was only slightly less. The prayer speeches of Mahatma Gandhi and Pandit Nehru's statements on the happenings in the East Punjab and Delhi have been so candid that phrases and sentences could be, and indeed were, torn out of their context and used as excellent propaganda by a section of the press in Pakistan and in America and Britain. Pandit Jawaharlal's broadcast on the Delhi riots was remarkable not only for its downright denunciation of non-Muslim rioters but for its discreet omission of any reference to the armed pockets in Muslim houses and quarters; it may have perplexed the local Hindus but Pandit Nehru evidently did not want to dilute his appeal with such qualifications which characterized the utterances of Pakistan's leaders and which are taken as self-justificatory by wrong-doers. The un-understanding opprobrium which was heaped on Gandhiji by refugees from the West Punjab probably exceeds in quantity the praise which all the world has showered on him in his long career. Yet, both Gandhiji and Pandit Jawaharlal Nehru, by remaining true to themselves, have also been true to their community and their country. They have courageously and consistently rejected the concept of competitive degradation and their temporary unpopularity will only be a foil to the recognition of their greatness in the fullness of time.

Jinnah and his followers have been victims not only of the circumstances but of the contradictions in their creed and method. Their two-nation theory spelt hatred, but hatred had to be worked up to a breaking point to force a division of the country. Their belated belief in the feasibility of constitutional safeguards for minorities in India and Pakistan could not be operative without a mixed administration which they had themselves destroyed. Their reasonableness on the eve of the partition could not at once convert followers and calm the minorities; it did not survive the first impact of the disturbances. They had been so used to pointless polemics that they continued the exercise when they should have jumped into the fray to end it. They had created in record time a fanatical following and a volunteer corps as good as a private army, but in the hour of crisis they had neither the will nor perhaps the strength to check their followers. The sins of the fathers are proverbially visited on their sons. Here is, however, an instance of Nemesis visiting politicians in the very hour of their triumph.

Chapter VIII

The Rout of the Minorities

Scientists experiment, observe and record results in the laboratory, before declaring their conclusions universally applicable; doctors watch the effects of drugs on rats before putting them on the market; surgeons operate on frogs and dead bodies before trying out new methods on human beings. Politicians are untrammelled by any such dilatory conventions and can straightaway, with a clear conscience, prescribe their nostrums to the millions. The 'surgical solution' of the minority problem in India had been advocated since 1940 by Mr. Jinnah; the first part of the operation was the carving of India into two parts and the second part was the removal of the residual minorities to the relevant part. Every surgeon who operates has to take risks; so must the politician who uses the surgical method. The patient may die on the table, but this is after all a part of the perils of the undertaking.

There were other doctors in the land who warned that this political surgery was arrant quackery, that it would kill the patient it professed to cure. Exchange of population had been tried in South-Eastern Europe after the First World War and had turned out to be a costly and incomplete system of treatment of the problem of minorities in a nation-state. Unfortunately, the facts of political history do not have the same relevance for a politician which case-histories have for medical men. The political surgeon was adamant; the country could be cut up, the minorities could be exchanged. Nevertheless, exchange of population was impracticable. The partition envisaged the creation of two sovereign States to serve as the 'homelands' of the two principal communities. The minorities in the proposed 'homelands'—many millions on both sides of the border—however, wished to believe and were made to believe that they would be able to live in security, even if without special privileges, after the political changes. The atmosphere was, of course, surcharged with tension but this appeared to be a passing phase. At any rate, there was no incentive—not even a compulsion yet— for sacrificing ancestral homes, habitations and occupations for the will-o'-the-wisp of a homeland. There was an exodus of non-Muslim minorities from the West Punjab districts to Hardwar and Patiala after the riots in March 1947, and from Lahore and Amritsar in the summer months; there was a reverse flight of Muslims from Amritsar. This exodus was far from being a migration; it was intended to be a temporary absence from the disturbed localities. There were hundreds of middle class Punjabi families who went to the hills or to other provinces to mark time till the restoration of peace in the Punjab. India's leaders told the people to stick to their homes and the same advice was given by the future rulers of Pakistan when they parted in the first week of August from their following in India.

A storm was anticipated in the critical days of the changeover of the Government in mid-August, but hopes were entertained that it would affect only a few localities and would soon blow over. I have been told an interesting story which reflects the faith of the saner section of the town dwellers on the eve of the partition. An anxious son wrote from Delhi to his old father at Mandi Bahauddin, a West Punjab small town, pleading with him to shift to Delhi for the uncertain month of August. He received the following reply:

> We have been born and brought up in these parts, whatever name they may get, whether Pakistan or Hindustan. I trust there will be no trouble at Mandi Bahauddin, but if there is, we will shift to Dinga and stay with your maternal uncle there.

Dinga is about 15 miles from Mandi Bahauddin and the simple old soul thought that this distance was sufficient to insulate a town from the communal contagion in a neighbouring town. There is no doubt that so long as there was a reasonable chance of peaceful conditions being maintained, there could be no exchange of population. In the Indian context, with the large numbers involved and the wide admixture of the population, there could be only a flight or (as it turned out) a 'rout' of the minorities. Jinnah once compared himself to the man who first used an umbrella; the ignorant opposition and ridicule to a great new idea finally turned to universal acceptance. Unfortunately, the trouble with Mr. Jinnah's umbrellas—'exchange of population' for instance—has been that they failed to open out at critical times; and in the meanwhile death, destruction and desolation rained upon a wide area.

The flight of the minorities, in those dark days of August 1947, to refugee camps or onto the roads leading to the frontier, enacted a tragedy beyond the power of words to describe. Sudden and overwhelming violence descended upon the minority communities at different places on both sides of the border, but there was no quantitative relationship between the violence and the panicky flight which it started. In the popular mind the division of the country was synonymous with communal rule. The declaration of the Boundary Commission Award shook the confidence of the minority which found itself in the 'others' homeland'; physical violence only completed the process of demoralization. Even though defence was difficult, particularly in the case of the partiality of the police and the military, the minorities, in most cases, did not even try to hold on to their 'pockets'. Like a lightning flash it came to them that the game was up; everything seemed alien to them, the civil administration, the police and the army; even their house frightened them as a potential prison or a slaughterhouse; the assassin's knife was receiving a fresh edge on the stone; the fire-raising brigade might be at the door any minute. As the instinct of self-preservation was roused, the attachment to earthly possessions suddenly became atrophied. The definition of a secular state and the charters of minority rights were just dangerous nonsense to those who felt themselves in deadly peril.

In the countryside, an anxious call pierced the still summer air like a fire bell in the night. 'To the border!' In the twinkling of an eye, an interminable queue of carts and cattle, men, women and children formed on the road leading to the frontier. Some of those who fled in such stunning haste got a grim goodbye. There were ambushes on road convoys and trains, at the end of which a lot of luggage, a few cattle and some women were found missing and the ground was strewn with a few dead bodies. It must be admitted that the milk of human kindness did not dry up all at once. There were extraordinary instances where neighbourly attachment was not shaken by popular passion or even the fear of the mob. I have heard of men and women who were hidden under haystacks or cold ovens by kind neighbours. I can picture the scene when the hooligans arrived to check up; the beating hearts in the oven and the haystack must have stilled as the assassins suspiciously scoured the place for the 'condemned' men; the protectors, perhaps a little pale, are likely to have put on a considerable amount of bravado and righteous indignation at not being taken at their word. Such steadfastness was, however, the exception because the hooligans were better organized and better armed than the majority of peaceful citizens in villages and towns; neighbours are generally kind folks but not of the stuff of which martyrs are made.

Of this period it has been said that human life was very cheap. The truth, however, is that life was never held at a higher ransom. All carriers, tonga drivers, taxi-owners, rickshaw coolies and even unlicensed street porters had a roaring trade. One trip with the refugees or with their kit was equal to an ordinary month's earnings. The 'traffic constable' at the public crossing was busier than ever before; he was there to prevent accidents and how could he be sure that there was no dangerous article in the bag under the lady's arm or in the steel trunk under the seat? If the traffic constable charged a small fee for making only a perfunctory search he could not be blamed. Then, there were the formalities of buying tickets and securing accommodation at the railways station. The booking clerk looked hard at the passengers and recognized the refugees who were deserting to a foreign country. He explained that the fares printed on the tickets were out of date, and then the journey was not an ordinary one; it was a race for life—or perhaps to death. The ticket collector at the gate was a poor man with a large family and could only admit those onto a crowded platform who were prepared to pay a special surcharge. Finally, the guard of the train remembered the mandatory clause of the Railways Act against overloading of carriages and travelling on footboards; for jeopardising the safety of all the passengers he felt quite justified in recovering an adequate premium from the refugees to cover the entire risk. It was the same story at the aerodrome. There were wholesale-dealers who had chartered a plane from Delhi and sold the seats to the fleeing refugees at the cost price plus a reasonable interest on the invested capital. Some refugees who had evidently never travelled by an aeroplane appeared to think that an air passage carried with it the right to carry a cart-load of household effects; they were made to surrender the excess weight of jewellery, silk clothes and currency to customs and police officials who were assisting the aerodrome officials in keeping order on the ground and preventing a crash in the air. There was a strange irony in this situation in which a refugee squandered the remnants of his life-savings in a bid to save his life.

At long last the journey to the border began. In the aeroplane it was so short that as the refugee landed on friendly soil he felt as if he had abruptly woken up from a nightmare. The journey by rail was long, more arduous and more hazardous. Trains were overcrowded as they had never been before; the interior of the carriage was packed with human beings as if they were bags stacked in a goods wagon; the roof of the carriage resembled a plate full of candy with flies on it. Those who were leaving their home districts for good should not have been sorry if the train was slow, for their eyes could linger a little longer on the familiar landscape; but to the passengers this extraordinary rail journey was a race against time; they feared that the sands of time might run out before the wheels of the train completed their prescribed revolutions. Never had a passenger train crawled forward so reluctantly; the coal was bad; the water made poor steam; the engine was in bad repair; the fireman was sick or the driver had done the maximum number of hours a heartless railways administration could exact from him. The train had prescribed halts at stations and also 'out-of-course' halts between stations. If it had a military escort the troops needed all their vigilance to keep off raiders. If it was unescorted (as in the first few days) the passengers had no option but to fend for themselves and to face those experiences, the dread of which had driven them from their homes.

The countryside was dotted with foot convoys which trailed along for miles on the roads to the frontier. From a high altitude or from a distance these caravans may have resembled a mediaeval army on the march. On a closer view, however, these columns appeared to lack both the buoyancy of a victorious army and the desperate energy of a retreating rabble. Men, women and children, even the cattle, stared as they trudged along. There was no anger and no vindictiveness on their faces—not yet; they moved forward as if they wore leaden shoes. The endless journey may have been tiring, but the fatigue somehow added to the chill of the nights under the sky. Mentally these people were numb. Had it been an avalanche or an earthquake and not the handiwork of man, they may have more easily reconciled themselves to the miseries. Again and again one question gnawed at their soul: 'Why has this happened—Why, Why, Why?' It was the eternal question of the agonized individual of flesh and blood to the decrees of cold-blooded politics.

In a moving mass of uprooted humanity, an old Muslim refugee halted on the Ferozepore Road at Lahore and asked a passer-by: 'Brother, how far is Pakistan from here?' Half an hour later she entered a refugee camp run by private charity and Government support. There must be hundreds of thousands of simple souls who crossed the frontier into their 'homelands' and were similarly conducted to refugee camps.

Chapter IX

Mental Rehabilitation

A refugee camp may be a feat of organization with thousands of tents, with electricity and water laid on, bustling officials and volunteers. Nevertheless, it is a poor substitute for the rude hamlet or the homely little town; it lacks the old familiar faces, the corner of the mud-hut, the fresh water from the village well; and even the flickering flame of the mustard-oil earthen lamp gave more warmth than the strange dazzle of the electric light.

Those who run the 'camp' may be able to supply sorely needed food, clothing and shelter to the inmates; but they cannot as easily heal their pain. The refugees, many of whom have drained the cup of sorrow to the dregs, have tragic tales to tell. I once chanced upon a well-educated middle-aged person, who had lost everything in the riots, his wife and all his five children. He told me that he had questioned hundreds of thousands of refugees passing through that town but he had met none so unfortunate as himself. There was a strange pathos in this grim boast of one who considered himself 'Misfortune's Favourite'! Nor can I forget the scenes I saw on the main road of a flooded border town in the East Punjab. A young mother with her little child was crying to the heavens as her dead husband lay in her lap. Presently all was silence; a sweeper came and collected the dead body and added it to the pyre on the road-side. On that awful night of 28th September, when the river Sutlaj ran amuck and flooded Ferozepore, I found a family of eight refugees in a public square, who could not flee to safety as others had done, because one of the boys had not returned from the town; I often wonder how the cruel dilemma was resolved; whether one member was written off to save the rest or—as in the common drowning tragedy—all the family in a vain attempt to save one, immolated themselves in a watery grave.

For many of those who survive, life is a burden which drags them down. The unfamiliar pangs of poverty are bitter indeed. To wake up one morning and find yourself a pauper is a shocking discovery. The ephemeral nature of the material world and the volatility of wealth have been popular beliefs or perhaps superstitions in this country, but in practice they have been more a consolation for the dying than a support for those condemned to live. The loss of land and buildings and earning capacity may be grievous, but it is not so galling from hour to hour as the deprivation of those little possessions which are the real luxuries of life—the personal clothing, the books, precious letters, the old family album and so on.

If the impact of sudden bereavement combined with sudden impoverishment unhinges its victim, it is no matter for surprise. I have anxiously searched in trains and trucks and streets for an expression of grim realism among the refugees but in most cases I have been disappointed. The commonest expression is that of expressionlessness; a face which has the pallor of death, staring eyes which do not see, legs which have the gait of automatons. By contrast, a few refugees display a striking and indeed suspicious liveliness; they argue long and hard, they think nothing of their losses, and would take their revenge 'here and now'. This pugnacity is, however, essentially 'escapist' in origin—a reaction from deep despair. The refugees will be themselves again neither through bottomless despair nor through false bravado—both of these attitudes arise from a fear of facing the full blast of tragedy in the open.

'We are healed by suffering', wrote Marcel Proust, 'only by experiencing it to the full'. To dam the grief is to let it fester inside; to forget and to forgive may be a good maxim in political controversy, but in mental hygiene, it is better not to forget the wrong and yet to forgive the wrongdoer. The irreconcilability of grief is a necessary stage in its experience. It cannot be skipped; it has to be lived through before the further stages of resignation and acceptance are traversed.

If I had anything to do with the running of the refugee camps, I would give no less attention to looking after the mental outfit of the refugees than to their physical needs. A large proportion of men and women in these camps spend almost all their waking hours pining for what was and is no more. Will it not be more economical to collect these people every day for one hour and let them have from a practised preacher a graphic description of their grief and the full magnitude of their tragedy so as to rip open their wounds until the ground was wet with tears? The rest of the day would then be spent in less sterile but more useful occupations, small tasks which at once exercise the body and prevent the mind from rambling.

The works of the Russian novelist Dostoevsky have a recurring thesis—the essential role of suffering in life. He believed that men did not acquire humility until they had suffered some humiliation, and could not know the strength of goodness unless they had themselves borne the impact of evil. His own condemnation to death and imprisonment in Siberia 'struck him as the greatest of mercies and it was in Siberia that he learnt the great lesson of his life'. Of his arrival in Siberia he has written:

Arrived, we stayed herded together by the door—
that is to say, in the lowest place of all—and as
I stood there, there came back to me the reflection
how when in church during the days of my
boyhood, I had been wont to gaze at the common
people near the entrance and to feel that somehow

they must be praying in a different way from ourselves—that they must be praying in a more humble, more grovelling fashion and with a fuller sense of their abasement. And now it had befallen me to stand in the very same place as they had done—albeit with this difference that I and my companions stood there cowed and fettered. Everyone in the church drew away from us, as if they were afraid of us; yet at the same time we were given alms, and I remember that somehow the circumstance communicated to me a sort of pleasure and something subtly resembling a sense of relief.

Dostoevsky's belief was not just the aberration of an artist. 'Shock-therapy' is an essential instrument of the psycho-analyst for the reconditioning of neurotic personalities. Experience imparts its slow wisdom to the average human being but this wisdom is often attained too late and at too great an expense in terms of happiness. For the neurotic the bargain is indeed very hard; he has paid down too much for too little, and his mind cannot grasp the full extent of his loss though it is confused and uneasy. The psycho-analyst sets out to lay bare before his patient the black mark of the neurosis; he strings together the tangled chords of the patient's past history and adds to them further strands of the same stuff, which would form in the future. The sight of his own product with the naked eye shocks the patient, unhinges him. The patient has seen the stuff of his life with all its coarseness and its knots, disowns it and, under the careful guidance of the psycho-analyst, is enabled to try newer and better patterns. The psycho-analyst, therefore, uses the element of shock to destroy the self-deceptions, the false security, the improvised hide-outs of the patient. This is a destructive process but it enables the psycho-analyst to clear the debris and make it possible for the patient to rebuild his personality on more enduring foundations. Even when shock is not the stratagem of a physician but the outcome of the malevolence of man or nature, it has its educative value.

Adversity is a good school but it can teach only those who have the capacity and the will to learn. There are many people in the Punjab who have known better days and who like Dostoevsky find themselves on the wrong side of the threshold. Dostoevsky in the moment of his humiliation learnt humility; he received a new insight into poverty and suffering; his sympathies were enlarged. Others may learn the same lessons provided they want to. If experience is (to quote Arthur Helps) the extract of sufferings, the sufferers of the Punjab have had jars full of the costly liquid. Those who have turned paupers overnight could hardly recover that itch for money-making on which black markets flourish. Those who have buried or cremated their dead on the roadside and slept in the midst of stink need no lessons on the dignity of labour and the virtues of cleanliness. Those who have witnessed and suffered the extremes of human brutality, and have shared suffering with thousands, need no sermons on fellow-feeling. And finally, those who have experienced mob rule against themselves should not dream of allowing it to be repeated in the province of their adoption—even against others.

Adversity is a good school but unfortunately few people have the courage or the wisdom to graduate from it. The great majority of people do not learn humility from humiliation or distil goodness from evil. Calamities pass over them like a summer storm, and their memories are as short as those of the Bourbons who returned to France after years of exile, having learnt nothing and forgotten nothing.

Chapter X

The Administrative Problem

The mass evacuation of the minorities from the West to the East Punjab involving millions was, to quote Sardar Patel, the 'greatest rescue project' in history. It was owing to ceaseless planning from the highest to the lowest governmental level, a gigantic organizational effort, steady perseverance in the face of incalculable obstacles and gusts of popular passions that a task which in the middle of August had appeared well-nigh impossible was completed. Though the successful evacuation of the minorities is rightly a matter for satisfaction to those who shared in this great and difficult enterprise the time for self-congratulation has not yet arrived. There is a danger that with no such spur as 'SOS' signals from those on the other side of the border, for whom 'precious hours were wearing away', the sense of urgency may wane and the Government and the people lapse into a premature complacency. We have not yet seen the end of this problem; not even the end of its beginning.

That the distressed refugees should look up to the Government is only to be expected. The connection of the disturbances with the political decisions which preceded them, the extent of loss of life and property, and the vast problems of relief and rehabilitation made it obvious from the outset that the infant East Punjab Province had neither the resources nor the organization to meet the crisis. All-out aid was, however, pledged by the Central Government from the first. There is a whole repertoire of arguments which seek to establish the direct responsibility of the Government of India towards the refugees. These arguments are unnecessary since those who are already convinced need no further persuasion. Some of these arguments are, nevertheless, interesting and provide a peep into the minds of the refugees. It is argued, and rightly, that the evacuation has been a direct, though perhaps an unexpected, result of the partition of the country and hence the Government of India, composed of the leaders who accepted the partition, have a moral obligation to the refugees. It is also argued that the minorities in the Punjab, N.W.F.P. and Sind have paid the price for the freedom of the provinces and states which constitute the present Indian Union: the Muslim League's pound of flesh was taken from the ribs of the non-Muslim minorities of the provinces which were formed into Pakistan. I have also heard what I may call the argument of parental responsibility of the state, which incidentally was recognized in the ancient Indian monarchy, in the benevolent autocracy of the Mughal Kings and the early parental (*Mai Bap*) misconception of the British officers in India. The refugees' claim to be the children of India who have been disinherited for no fault of theirs and must now be settled again. The professional and business classes, who have suffered heavy losses, contend that it is for the Government to make up for these; according to this reasoning the Government is assumed to be an insurance company with 'all risks policies' for every citizen, thus carrying an obligation to reimburse the refugees for their losses to the last pie. An insurance company is, however, based upon the actuarial incidence of risks and is even less able than a bank to survive a 'run' on it. If a large number of policy-holders of a life insurance company, with malicious intent to ruin the fortunes of the directors, commit suicide, the insurance company's directors almost certainly would face bankruptcy. Similarly, if a fire insurance company is asked to pay the claims to policy-holders in a burnt town where it had a host of clients, it will either wriggle out with the help of a nice point of law, or close shop. In a sense, a modern democratic state is an insurance company but it covers only the minimum risks for the poorest sections. Such an explanation is cold comfort to those who have been stripped of their property and belongings. The simplest and the most equitable arrangement would appear to be for Pakistan and India to pay compensation to evacuees from their respective territories but this is hardly likely to be accepted by Pakistan since it would only increase Pakistan's debt to India. Nor is it likely that the refugees would get adequate compensation for what they left behind even through the 'custodians' appointed by the Government. For one thing, the movable property may have already moved away before the custodian came on the scene. For another, the market price of the immovable property depends upon the interplay of demand and supply. The scarcity of land and houses is not so acute in the West Punjab as in the East Punjab and there are comparatively fewer people with surplus liquid capital. The auctions, even if they could be conducted fairly in the absence of the owners, would not fetch anything like the market price before 15th August, 1947. There is little doubt that many of the displaced persons will have to make the best of a bad bargain and to cut their losses.

The Finance Minister of India in his last budget made a provision for nearly 27 crores for the 'relief and rehabilitation' of refugees in the East Punjab. This sum may fall short of the expectations and the needs of the refugees, whose losses in terms of real estate and property of all kinds have been so heavy, that even if the rest of India went on a five years' fast and all the revenues were mortgaged to rehabilitation work in the East Punjab, there would remain quite a number of displaced persons whose fortunes would still be unrepaired. There is a certain *naivete* in measuring rehabilitation only in terms of the crores spent. In the budget parlance, this expenditure is a subvention from the Centre to a Province; in the language of economics it is a subsidy; in less euphemistic language it is a dole. Subsidies and doles, unless given in small and measured doses, tend to prolong the disease which they are intended to cure.

The effectiveness of the relief organization set up by the Government depends not only upon its size and scope but also upon the spirit informing it. Tent-cities for the refugees have been set up through the agency of the State; the problem had outrun the resources of the philanthropic organizations. Nevertheless, the civil servant in a refugee camp is just a square peg. He is trained to plan, to build and to expand; in his hands the midget of a Stores Department can grow into the monster of the Supply Department. A refugee camp, however, like Marx's (not Stalin's) 'Proletarian State', must function so as to make itself dispensable and finally to go into self-liquidation. The word 'refugee' like the word 'untouchable' jars upon sensitive ears. The refugee camp would have fulfilled its function if it created an atmosphere in which this word becomes one of reproach; the camp is not a place where, in return for modest comforts of food, clothing and shelter, the residents have time for self-pity or day-dreaming; it is a place where freed from stark cold and hunger they acquire the incentive and have the opportunities to redeem inch by inch their self-esteem and their self-reliance.

A satisfactory solution of the refugee problem depends on the appreciation of the magnitude and complexity of the problem by the whole body of administrators from the base of the pyramid right up to the ministerial apex. The East Punjab imported a trained administrator for its governorship but it cannot import ministers and leaders of public opinion from outside. The fertile soil of the Punjab had for years no exotic plants like Nehru, Patel, Rajagopalachari, Pant and others. In the East Punjab government and politics there are probably many good men but hardly a great one. This is not intended to be uncomplimentary to anybody; no one has yet been hauled up before the court of law or the bar of public opinion for failure to attain the attributes of greatness. Indeed, it is in the interest of those upon whom greatness is thrust to be conscious of the fact. In a nascent democracy in normal times, ministers learn by trial and error. In the East Punjab, with its problems of wartime urgency, there is, however, hardly a margin for error: a staff college cannot be opened in the trenches or as a Punjabee proverb puts it, 'One cannot dig a well when one is dying of thirst.' Brilliant and outstanding leadership has no adequate substitute; its loss can be partly made up by the team work of a diligent and competent group of men, conscious of their great responsibilities and great opportunities and their limitations.

Ministers function through civil servants scattered all over the country. The transition from an irresponsible alien rule to a self-governing democracy in a matter of a few months necessarily has forced on public servants a severe exercise in adaptation of outlook.

The heritage from the past has been not of the best. In the Punjab there was much nepotism and patronage under the Unionist rule; while other provinces in India may have had an opportunity of attacking these evils after the introduction of provincial autonomy, in the Punjab these evils were the pillars of the Unionist regime. The short innings of the Khizr-Sachar-Swarn Singh team did not make much of a difference. The disturbances after the partition of the province created fresh complications. During the first few days of lawlessness, a number of people succumbed to the temptation of feathering their own nests, until the heavy hand of the law made the fear of punishment greater than the temptation. The process of rehabilitation has its own pitfalls for the unwary or unscrupulous official. There is hardly a servant of the state in the East Punjab, who does not have a distressed relative, a friend, or a friend's friend knocking at his door for sympathy and help. Indeed, it would appear that many refugees choose to prefer their claims on the state through the proper channel—of the nearest relative or friend in a department. 'Personal' or 'family rehabilitation' is bound, however, to retard, warp and stunt national rehabilitation. There never was a time when public servants had greater difficulties in steering between political patronage and personal pressure but the need for persevering in the narrow path was also never greater.

The Indian Civil Service was popularly known as the 'steel frame' of British rule in India. The phrase 'steel frame' is generally applied to the members of the Indian Civil Service, the Indian Political Service, the Indian Police and the other Central services which manned the chief executive jobs in the Secretariat and in the districts. The British rule being at an end, it is a nice question as to whether the cold 'steel frame' can be transformed into a live wire. The transformation is dependent not only upon the malleability of the civil servants but also on the possibility of getting the proper current from the two ends, namely, a policy-framing and non-meddling ministry and an awakened but responsible public opinion. It goes without saying that the public servants will have to educate themselves for their role in the new order by breaking down the barriers which divided them from the common run of mankind; new traditions will grow, a new *esprit de corps* will have to take the place of a closed caste. The civil servant is only, however, one of a trio in which he occupies the middle position; in the language of the market place he is a retailer between the wholesaler (ministry) and the consumer (the public). Education into the new order is not only necessary for the civil servant but also for the politician and the public. It is not enough to ask the servants of the Government to become the servants of the people; it is excellent advice in itself and pertinent for those who were brought up in a different system. Yet, there is an assumption underlying the advice that the public has mastered the difficult art of acting as a master— which is not the case at present. Many grievances of the public are genuine but there are also difficulties even for the honest and diligent officials, which the public do not appreciate and it is not unoften that the refusal of a special concession or a particular favour is bruited abroad as a gross injustice. Corruption in government departments has been continued through collusion at public expense between corrupt officials and greedy non-officials. It is a vicious circle. An alien bureaucratic rule 'untouched by hand' (as Tagore put it) killed the initiative and the civic sense in the people and this result in its turn encouraged, if encouragement was needed, an arrogant, bossy and domineering attitude among many public servants. The vicious circle has to be broken, but it will need simultaneous breaks in the two arcs of the circle.

The disproportionate importance attached to the services in India in the past both by the Government and the public has been the target of much criticism and ridicule. The outlook of the brighter student was entirely moulded by the prospects of success at the examination at 'Metcalfe House' in Old Delhi, and promising boys from the universities were lost to routine jobs which promised a 'secure' career. Pandit Jawaharlal Nehru has referred in his *Autobiography* to the habit of self-congratulation and self-importance among members— British and Indian—of the I.C.S. Most of these men had the blessings of a university education and could boast of an above-the-average academic career. They chose the career of the Civil Servant for the pay and prestige it carried, and with a desire to settle down; and generally they succeeded in settling down as a ship settles down.

In most cases, it was the system and not the men who were to blame. A few months ago *The Statesman* published an article bearing the title 'Forty Years Behind the Times' which showed how far the secretariat of the Government of India was outmoded in its organization and methods. The national leaders who have exchanged their prison cells for the seats of power have shown an extraordinary indulgence to those who served as instruments, willing, in some cases, of the British repressive machinery. The best that can be said for the Indian members of the 'steel frame' is that the political role was forced on them by their position and by the necessity of saving a career to which there was no comparable alternative outside the wings of the Government. The new entrants to a profession are generally moulded by its traditions. The same Englishman who would have accepted a quiet and anonymous existence in the Home Civil Service turned out, on joining the Indian Civil Service, to be a minor Robert Clive. Ultimately, the civil servants in this country will have to approximate to the circumscribed and anonymous role of the civil servant in Britain, thus becoming the obedient instruments of a responsible ministry, faithfully interpreting its desires and executing its policies, in a manner which is satisfactory to the public and entails the least friction for themselves. It must be borne in mind that the present position of the English Civil Service is due to historical reasons and to traditions which have been developed over a period of time. There is nothing inexorable in the growth of these traditions; many executive jobs in the states of North America are a part of the political plums which fall to the winners of an election. If the civil servant in Britain is in his proper place it is because of the pressure of the right amount and quality applied to him from the top as well as from the bottom. In Britain there have been stray scandals implicating ministers of the State, but as a rule, the level of public life has been creditably high; side by side with this freedom from gratuitous meddling by politicians in the details of administration a useful check is provided by public opinion, which has local and generally effective channels of expression.

There is one pitfall for the senior civil servants in India, which it would be well for them to avoid. During the last twenty years, the British officers had to admit Indian officers as colleagues, sometimes as bosses; but there were certain top jobs, the strategic points which they could not surrender before a total evacuation. Many of these jobs have now been made available to Indians. A drastic reshuffle of the services took place in August; many Europeans retired to England, and most of the Muslims opted for rule in Pakistan. In this process, quite a few have gained; the appetite, however, grows with what it feeds on; many people would like the elevator to move up quickly; first floor, second floor, third floor—and finally top floor, from where one can look down upon the little dwarfs who once presumed to rub shoulders with him.

The unassuming and comparatively modest role of a civil servant in England has its own compensations;

it may hurt the *amour propre* of those who were once members of the 'heaven-born' services, but makes lesser demands on the individual who is expected to draft minutes and execute policies, with few occasions for much self-assertion. Similarly, the proud pose of a 'Burra Sahib' was caught easily—like a cold—from the British colleague. The administrative problem in the East Punjab—and perhaps in the whole of India—is in many ways somewhat raw; it calls for not only bold political leadership, but for great enterprise, intelligence and tact from those who apply the national policies to the masses. Neither the hauteur of the 'Burra Sahib,' nor the self-effacement of a British civil servant, can carry the Indian officers through the next few years. They need something of the adventure and personal integrity of the early British administrators like John Lawrence and Charles Metcalfe and something of the burning faith of the lieutenants of Lenin who after the Russian Revolution hammered order out of chaos.

The executive officers in India, as elsewhere, function through a large body of smaller officials dispersed in the districts. If the higher services were the 'steel frame' of British rule in India, the smaller officials were the tenuous but tough wire gauze which netted—as in a vice—the countryside. Without much education and perhaps because of this, they cultivated overweening self-importance and enlightened self-interest in an ample measure. Their tenure and prospects did not rest on their good behaviour towards the public, but on the good opinion of the 'Sahib' in the district; their power—often abused for petty tyranny—was proportional to the distance from the district headquarters. The habit of obedience to the 'Sahib' was generally hereditary; British bayonets may have been the ultimate fear, but to all intents and purposes the Briton's face was quite as effective. Such a large class of officials containing thousands of men is not easy to re-educate, but without a reorientation of its outlook the peasantry and the small-town dweller cannot have the fruits of political freedom. During the War and in 1946-47—the year of riots—and in the process of a two-way exodus of minorities in the Punjab, the discipline and integrity of some of the lower public officials have considerably deteriorated. To put these men in their proper places will be the additional responsibility of the higher executive; if circulars and lectures fail, the application of severe disciplinary measures will be the only alternative.

A new outlook in all ranks of the hierarchy is the prime need of the hour. New methods of working are partly linked up with the new outlook, but in many ways they will help to hasten its growth. The British in India kept the peace in India—but did little more. Their administration was beautifully designed to preserve the *status quo.* There was such a successful structure of wheels within wheels, that nothing novel or dangerous could come out of it. A third division clerk set the ball rolling by writing a note on a subject of national importance; the file kept on moving, like a bad coin, collecting the footnotes of the whole departmental hierarchy. The Secretariat and district officials did what they must, and for the rest, they would let others alone, if they themselves were also shown the same consideration. All this has changed. It is no longer possible even to presume the *status quo*. There are scars of the War which have not healed and the ravages of the riots which have to be repaired. Our administration is, however, not a darning, mending or repair shop; it has to build up the entire economy of the country on sound foundations. An office file is no more an exercise book where the members of one or more departments can enter into a competition with one another on writing a piece of English composition on a given subject. Decisions cannot wait; the waiting is expensive in terms of public welfare.

Some wagons containing the records of the East Punjab Government which were booked from the West Punjab are reported to be missing. The East Punjab Government would do well to give up the search, not only to save the railway freight, but also in the interests of administrative efficiency. Precedents are to civil servants what crutches are to the lame; every step is to be sanctioned by the last note on the file, or by a back-reference to the previous note based on a quotation from an office manual, since out of print. Precedents contribute to continuity; but continuity is hardly an asset when one has to write virtually—as in the Punjab today—on a *tabula rasa*. The wanton destruction of office records and files by an ignorant mob may accomplish the happy result of substituting common sense for precedents in administration.

Chapter XI

Economic Rehabilitation and Regeneration

The flight of minorities across the northern Radcliffe line was due to political causes, but it has created an economic problem of unprecedented proportions and gravity. It is nothing less than the settlement of nearly 45 lakhs of evacuees from the West Punjab. These people have lost all their immovable property and in many cases their personal belongings. They have to be transplanted in the East Punjab or other provinces and assured shelter and livelihood.

If the movement of population between the two Punjabs after the partition of India had been something like an exchange or rather a barter, the problem would have been somewhat simpler, since a parity in numbers, possessions and occupations could have been attempted. As it is, the West Punjab province in Pakistan is short of business and professional talent while the East Punjab in India has excess of both. It has been stated that the Hindus and Sikhs in the West Punjab vacated 70 lakhs of acres of land while the Muslim evacuees from the East Punjab vacated only 30 lakhs of acres. (These figures given by Master Tara Singh have not been contradicted.) As regards housing, there are no reliable statistics, but the number and quality of houses vacated in the West Punjab are vastly superior to those vacated in the East Punjab. This shortage of land and houses ultimately limits the capacity of the East Punjab province to absorb all those who have come to it for succour.

It is inevitable that some of the refugees will have to spill over to the neighbouring provinces. The United Provinces have, however, already banged the door against refugees from the Punjab. This is to be set down not merely to parochial exclusiveness, but to the fear that the refugees may create in the U.P. the same anarchy from which they themselves had fled. A distressed refugee is, in his own way, a great leveller; he would, if he could, bring others down to his unfortunate level of privation. The East Punjab Government has done its duty in lodging a protest in the proper quarters against the ban imposed by the Government of the U.P. but the latter is not likely to relax the embargo until it feels sure of the good behaviour of the refugees. Here is a point of morals which hedges—some would say needlessly—the solution of an economic problem.

The neighbouring provinces, even if they throw their doors open, are not likely to take in more than a small number of refugees. Most of the Punjabis would themselves hate to go away from a region where they are freer than elsewhere to live their own lives, meet their own people and blaspheme in their own dialect. It is, moreover, expected that the East Punjab Government is likely to develop economically with the centrally financed projects of irrigation and electrification; and the East Punjab Premier the other day publicly expressed the hope that many of those whom the East Punjab had to send away for the time being may be able to return later. I am not qualified to judge the full potentialities of the Nangal and Bhakra projects; nor do I want to underrate the expected benefits from them. It seems to me, however, that the popular view of these projects is almost romantic. The Nangal and Bhakra schemes after all are not just an 'open sesame' to the portals of prosperity; they are engineering projects, which will take time to be completed (particularly after the reported flight of the Pathan contractor who fled to Pakistan with his hundreds of stone cutters and lakhs of mules) and even when the work is completed, its full benefits will not be reaped for two or three years.

The problem of rehabilitation cannot pend for two or three years; it cannot wait even for three months. The province has no option but to make the best use of the available resources. For the next few months, or perhaps years, it would be essential to grow the maximum crops to feed more people; and the old mud-houses must be repaired or new ones put up without waiting for the bricks, steel and cement which are in any case in short supply all over the world—with the exception of the U.S.A. To those who have left 'squares' of fertile lands and rows of fine buildings in the West Punjab, the East Punjab may not be able to offer very satisfactory substitutes but they will perforce make a start on a smaller, but perhaps a cleaner, state.

In economic reconstruction, as in mental rehabilitation, the breakdown of the ruling system is often an opportunity for rearing a healthier structure. The press has published the good news that the Government of India has already decided to experiment in agrarian reform on the lands that are being allotted to the West Punjab refugees; the Director-General of the Rehabilitation Departments is a civil servant who has written a thoughtful little book bearing the self-explanatory title *Poverty and Social Change*. A book on Indian economics is likely to find a place only on the bookshelves of the poor professors who are required to keep abreast of new books to protect themselves from surprise attacks in the classroom from post-graduate students. Most of the upper class and middle class families for their political and economic—and indeed literary—knowledge depend upon their daily newspapers and the news bulletins relayed from the nearest radio station.

Unfortunately a book on the 'Rape of the Punjab' would sell out before the Government has had time to publish its edict of proscription, but a book on 'Rape Seeds' or on 'Collective Farming' will go on collecting dust in the book shop until the *ex officio* buyers, the librarians or the professors, turn up. The district officers who run the revenue administration in many cases have never read such subjects as economics, and even if it formed part of their curriculum at the university they may not remember much even out of the text-book generalizations. As for the smaller officials, books on Collective Farming or Capitalist Farming have no more relevance for them than books on Astronomy. The Government can, of course, fill up the gaps in the education of its staff by issuing circulars; the Director-General can and does issue general directives. The trouble about circulars, however, is that while many people help to draft them, there is only one person at a time to read and digest them, and I am not revealing a secret if I say that quite a few circulars from the Secretariat to the subordinate offices are duly received, formally acknowledged and neatly filed—but seldom read.

Agrarian reform is, however, something more than a problem of revenue administration; it is something more than even an economic policy; it calls for a new way of life, a new *weltanschauung*. What is required is not broad acres with all the male adults toiling on them 'according to plan'; the object is a new organic unit, a renovated village community, with a corporate sense of its own, combining a balance of occupations with a harmony of human relationships and containing within self seeds for further growth.

The village was once a self-contained unit; its community within its slender resources was economically self-sufficient, and virtually self-governing. Owing to historical reasons, the old village community lost its self-sufficiency and much of its vitality. What was a historical truth is no longer a fact. Whatever has survived of the corporate feeling is the least evident in the attitude to land. The peasant from tradition and belief is the strongest protagonist of private ownership of land. The laws of inheritance provided for equal division of land among the brothers; how could the right of primogeniture work in a community which had few alternative outlets for the younger brothers? In the process of division, the brothers shared among themselves not only the area but also bits of the best land in the patrimony; the result was the emergence of a jigsaw puzzle of small and scattered fields which were progressively fragmented with each bequest until many of the holdings were so small, that a family and a pair of bullocks did not get a full day's work; there was thus neither an incentive for, nor any advantage in, trying out better methods of cultivation. The fragmentation of the fields is thus as much a symbol as a cause of the fragmentation of the corporate tradition of the village community. The pressure of population added to the inherited hunger for land in an overcrowded economy where every bit of land figured as a source of badly-needed morsels of food for hungry mouths— which came thick and fast. With this background, the appetite grew until it became a passion. In the villages of the Punjab as also in some other provinces, land has become in the eyes of the villagers so dear that human life in comparison appears cheap. The records of criminal courts contain innumerable instances of land disputes, the upshot of which was broken heads and broken homes. If water from a canal channel in a peasant's field trickled into the neighbour's field, and it appeared to be no accident, the loss of water was often made up by a stream of blood. If cattle strayed into a neighbour's field, as cattle are wont to do, but if the peasant watching his crops flew into a rage, the muddy trail of the cow's feet was covered with the red blood of its owner. It is to such peasantry, tied by an inexpressible and hereditary passion to land, that a corporate agrarian economy has to be 'sold'; and 'sell' it must.

On collective farming, I have questioned several West Punjab refugees who are being settled in villages. Most of them have no precise ideas on the subject; they guess that it is something about land being owned by the Government and the villager sharing in cultivation and harvests; they hope that the scheme is just the townsman's brainwave and will not be put into operation, and they are sure that it will not work; they are unable to see any relation between their being uprooted and the necessity of adopting a system other than that they have left behind in the West Punjab. I may recall here an interesting conversation with a refugee who had been a prosperous peasant in the West Punjab; he had a fair-sized holding there and had served in the army in the First World War. I questioned him on the rehabilitation in the villages and asked for his own reactions. Naturally enough, he began by expatiating on the injustice of being allotted only one-fifth of the land he had owned in the West Punjab. I asked him about Collective Farming. 'Yes', he replied, 'the Government is asking for a minimum number of ploughs to be pooled. It may be a modern theory but it won't work'. 'Won't work?' I mechanically turned his last phrase into the next question. 'Yes, it won't because we people just cannot do it. If you have a family of ten and I have a family of three, why should I work as hard as you do? Moreover, if your children clip off an ear of corn each, mine must clip four each not to be losers in the bargain'. Here was the vexed problem of the incentive in a socialized economy though the old man could not put it that way. I did not want the conversation to end in a triumph for cornclipping individualism, and so I suggested that the spirit of working according to capacity and receiving according to need was not impossible to inculcate, and that some foreign countries had tried it. 'Yes, sir, it is said, they have done that in Russia, but it will take time here. Perhaps Gandhi may do it, if the riots cease and he can leave Delhi.'

In Russia, agriculture was collectivized—but at a cost. A whole class of *bourgeois* farmers, the *kulaks,* was 'liquidated'. Estimates of the death roll in this process of liquidation including the deaths caused by decreased production or by failure of the distribution organization vary, but some observers have given an eight-figure estimate. The nationalization of land and collective farming were achieved by the use of the whole coercive machinery of a powerful state, reinforced by the unremitting toil of the members of the majority party, in fact the only political party, in the Soviet Union, for whom State ownership of means of production has been a cult. While reorganizing our rural economy, we are free to adopt the way of persuasion, education and direction or to enforce a new way of life at the point of the sword. In the political sphere we have already seen the results of violence and of non-violence. A non-violent mass movement which continued for a quarter of a century, helped Britain and India to part in a spirit of goodwill unparalleled in the history of imperialism. A violent communal movement in one year has brought the whole of the subcontinent to a standstill, if not to the verge of a breakdown. If we permit agrarian or industrial anarchy to be superimposed upon communal anarchy, we are finished as a people. Non-violence is no longer a creed for the evolution of national unity and prosperity; it is not even a policy; it is an inescapable necessity.

In rural reconstruction, which embraces the happiness of eighty per cent of our population, we cannot afford the luxury of dogmas, nor try out 'soon-get-well' patents. Nationalization of land is an integral part of Socialist theory, and since few people deny allegiance to socialism (even Hitler had to call himself a National-Socialist), nationalization of land would appear to be the most modern panacea for all the ills of India's economy. Socialist theory, however, has to be applied to particular countries with some allowance for local conditions. In India in the present social and economic contexts, nationalization of land would appear to those peasants who own their land, or are about to secure the formal ownership from the landlord, as a scheme for depriving them, at one stroke, of the ancestral lands in the interest of an abstract entity called the state, represented in the village by the exacting *patwari* and the hated policeman. Abolition of private ownership in land is a policy which if not impossible in our country is at least premature. Abolition of the 'middlemen' who stand between the cultivator and the government is, however, a very desirable step, and most provincial governments are already taking action on it. As for the abolition of the zamindari, the zamindars have already nearly abolished themselves; their general lack of interest in their lands, their non-cultivating, and non-residential roles had left only one link between them and the land, in the form of rent; the tenants could always cut this link, particularly if the government refused to guarantee a link which was not beneficent to the land, to the peasant and even to the landlord. The disappearance of the zamindar from the scene in itself will, however, no more ensure the prosperity of the agrarian economy than the disappearance of the British from India will ensure the prosperity of India; in each case the exit of the extraneous matter from the body politic which could stand in the way of advance is just a step forward.

Agrarian economy in India has to be reconstructed; tenancy legislation will only be breaking the old shackles and enabling the peasantry to grow if they have the will and the institutional facilities for growth. In the East Punjab, the huge movement of minorities after the August upheaval has made rural reconstruction a problem of imperative urgency, which cannot be shirked, and which cannot be postponed; the problem has to be tackled, perfunctorily or thoroughly. The perfunctory way is the easier way; it has precedents in office files or (if office files are missing) in the memories of the officials. There used to be (and perhaps still exists) a department of Rural Reconstruction in the Punjab; its permanent head was a member of the Indian Civil Service, Mr. Brayne, who wondered, like Marie Antoinette, why people who could not get bread did not eat biscuits. Mr. Brayne, presumably in broken Hindustani or Roman English, gave a bagful of useful advice to the villagers: they should not burn cow dung; they must wipe their muddy feet on the threshold, if their houses had thresholds at all; they must avoid the glare of the sun either by buying sun-glasses or if they could not afford them, by staying indoors; they should have more fresh air through more ventilators and more windows. Indeed, it was all window-dressing, a presentable patchwork to prove to visiting Viceroys or foreign tourists how much interest a benevolent government was taking in renovating the village. The 'model' villages of the department remained unique models and did not inspire poor attempts at imitation. The department of Rural Reconstruction did yeoman service in training a number of officials in the art of propaganda, and they proved very useful later, in collecting war loans and recruits. And at critical times, the department provided suitable posts for I.C.S. officers who were too junior to be Commissioners and too senior to continue as Deputy Commissioners.

A rural reconstruction programme which is meant not for 'model' villages but for the hundreds and thousands of villages cannot be launched, and if launched, cannot be carried out, by departments of the government. The role of the state is there, but it is pertinent to define its limitations. The government alone can furnish the administrative framework; ensure at reasonable prices the supply of home-produced or imported fertilizers and, where necessary, machinery for power farming; produce in state farms fresh strains and new seeds for crops and plants; make available a minimum of medical aid to men and cattle and finally enact a framework of permissive legislation which can be readily applied as a legal stamp on the *fait accompli* of the renovated village community. Here I would draw the line for the state. The functions already enumerated will probably cost the state a good deal of expenditure but it may be short of the sums allocated in the Tata-Birla plan. There is something pathetic in the popular faith in state expenditure: when a busy clerk who has only time for skimming the headlines of the daily newspapers reads of plans in terms of crores of rupees, his heart jumps up; the prosperity appears to be so tangible that he feels he has already shared it to some extent. Since the days of lend-lease the United States has set the fashion for plans involving billions of dollars, and many people have begun to suspect that there is some mysterious relationship between the U.S.A.'s astronomical public expenditure and her prosperity. Countries which lack the self-sufficiency and economic resources of the United States as well as her technological advancement find it difficult to visualize the productive power on which all her prosperity hinges. An indiscriminate aid and a largesse are beyond our resources. A loan from the state should be a loan in a businesslike fashion, seeking a definite return in public welfare. India's prosperity whether in agriculture or in industry will not be uncovered miraculously from a 'plan' in terms of crores. It is not a simple problem of borrowing and spending; for public money lent in good faith has to be spent cautiously. Prosperity will come from the productive efficiency of the people in all walks of life, from a conscious and concentrated attack on poverty, from the maximum use of the existing techniques and from the exploitation of the new techniques when they become available. In the last analysis, economic regeneration is a problem of intellectual reorientation, economics is the handmaid of education.

There is one limitation from which the state suffers in India, which is not common to all countries and which may cease to operate in India after some time. I have already dealt with this limitation in the chapter on 'The Administrative Problem'. The 'officials', once the local 'residents' of the British Raj in the countryside, have been as little loved and as much feared as the

'Residents' of the Crown Representative in the courts of Indian States; the only difference was that the tyranny of the petty official was less subtle and more pervasive. A villager's attitude to the official of even a national government would for some time at least continue to resemble the reactions of a man whose first memory of a doctor was the application of a little 'Mendals Paint' to his little throat and whom, for years later, the sight of a doctor gave an uneasy feeling in the throat. The programme of reconstruction cannot, however, altogether exclude the officials. One may trust an amateur to teach geography to an adult education class; but to let him treat sick animals, would be unfair to the 'dumb driven cattle'. The veterinary and agricultural departments in particular will have to train and distribute their 'field demonstrators' in the village, but they will have to come not as tutors, but as friends and neighbours, and to propagate their ideas not through speeches at street corners but by the improved quantity and quality of the crops in the demonstration farms in the village itself.

The revival of village economy requires vital leadership, and owing to historical reasons the official agency cannot provide it. Could the zamindars take on the mantle of leadership? The question may look ridiculous at a time when the provincial governments have legislation underway for the abolition of landlordism in India. The zamindar in this last phase can, nevertheless, stage a comeback; having lost the legal sanctions for his 'superior' right of rent collection and petty tyranny, he could create popular sanctions for local leadership by a spirit of service. Many French landlords in the decade before the French Revolution took an enlightened interest in their self-liquidation; they could not save their estates, but many of them saved their reputations and political careers for a generation or more. The landed gentry of India, however, suffers from its past. The majority of the landlords cannot trace their genealogy beyond four or five generations and the founder of the 'House' was in all probability a lucky rent-collector who got the benefit of the doubt from unsuspecting English administrators, who saw India's land problems in the image of the eighteenth-century English land system. There are a few families who may be able to boast of descent from Mughal times, but the nobility of the Mughals with its life tenures of public office and personal property never had a chance to develop those traditions of individual initiative, economic independence and political ambition which distinguished the English landed gentry. The zamindars of India, as a class, have been fitted neither by tradition nor by training for leadership in local or national affairs. They disqualified themselves for the leadership in their own estates by adopting the businesslike attitude of a rent-collector, by failing through better agricultural methods and apparatus to improve the fertility of the land, by living away from those whose toil supported their high standard of life, by preferring the gay company of the towns to the modest comforts of rural leadership. Few sons of the landlords exposed themselves to the physical or mental strain entailed in staying at the universities; they were thus spared the knowledge of those subversive movements which questioned their ancestral eminence and prosperity, but they were also disabled from actively participating in progressive movements, in the political, economic and educational spheres.

Evidently the village community will have to discover its own leadership: indeed it will have to discover itself. The discovery is by no means easy. As I have already stated, the historic corporate life of the village community is in abeyance; it was meant for a particular socio-economic context; it cannot be revived in its original form; it is dormant though not dead. Foreign observers have often commented upon the apathy, the inertia, the born fatigue of our villagers. The political awakening in the country destroyed some of this lassitude; it was, however, negative in nature, a protest against foreign rule, a revolt against superior might. The attainment of political freedom is likely to dry up the springs of the peasant's roused energy; there is in fact a danger that the pent-up energy may seek unexpected channels in factional or communal strife. Those who guide agrarian movements among a simple but illiterate peasantry, cannot but remember that real progress is impossible with mere negatives. The exit of the Briton was essential for political freedom; the exit of the landlord may be inevitable for economic independence; but by themselves these two events do not so much guarantee economic progress as create the conditions in which progress can be made. A 'negative' movement has an interminable chain: after the Briton, the zamindar, after the zamindar, the *bania,* then the artisan, then the Muslim or Hindu or Sikh or Christian. The personification of the opposing forces makes them vivid to the mind of the average person; the white man and the landlord were tangible (insofar as they were occasionally seen from a distance) symbols of oppression; it is not so easy to seek symbols for prejudice and ignorance. A crazy friend of mine once presided over a meeting of the Hindus in the Hissar district during a period of communal tension and in his winding-up address shocked them by suggesting that the real enemies of the Hindus were not Muslims but mosquitoes. Now, it is easier to catch by the neck a Muslim (or a Hindu or Sikh, for that matter) than a mosquito against which neither the press nor the radio fulminates. Yet it is necessary to drive home to the people in this subcontinent that the mosquito is their worst enemy, and so is disease, and so are ignorance, prejudice and passion. I like to think that the Editor of the *Dawn,* who helped Jinnah in winning Pakistan with a sword-pointed pen, may yet write an editorial on the Mosquito as 'Enemy Number One' with the same vituperative concentration with which he wrote on the Mahatma as 'Enemy Number One'.

There would appear to be in the villages no sources for vital leadership which one can easily spot; this is not, however, a matter for discouragement, much less dismay. The people throw up their own leaders when a crisis comes, and somebody can bring home to them the naked peril of their position. In the summer and autumn of 1940, the British people felt this crisis over them; they revealed new reserves of courage, endurance and unity. In the 1942 'revolt' the peasantry in several districts found itself pitched against heavy odds which sought to grind them down; they hit back viciously to save themselves and in the process discovered a new strength in them. In the district of Satara, the 'Prati Sarkar' waged a two-front battle against the police and the hooligan hirelings of the police; not only did they beat off these petty oppressors but they governed themselves in an efficient, humane and progressive fashion, locally settling petty disputes, looking after the families of those comrades who were absconding or in prison, abolishing caste, banning early marriages. Once again it was proved that if the common people were driven to the wall, they could fight with their back to the wall. It may, however, happen that a people may already have been driven to the wall, but may be almost ignorant of the fact. A peril is none the less for not being represented by bullying policemen and harassing hooligans, or by an invasion-fleet or air-armada. The straits in which the refugees of the Punjab and to a lesser extent the people of India find themselves today are probably worse than those in which the people of Britain found themselves in 1940. And, unfortunately, we are not even half as aware of our peril as the British people were. It is good to have faith in the destiny of one's race: the British people had it in the summer of 1940, but they had something more too—the will to resist, to fight and to win. In combating the heavy odds of poverty, disease, ignorance and now communal passion, we need in increasing measure the will to resist, to fight, and to win. The peril is around us, the stakes are high and the time short, but if our leaders and our publicists could only make an appeal in the Churchillian style for fighting poverty in the fields and factories, and ignorance in schools and offices, our survival and our future as a great nation may still be assured.

How are the masses of India to be roused to the urgency of their problems and how are they to be urged to discover themselves? There is no question of uplifting them; that is an outmoded patronizing phrase; they have only to be made to see that they are down, and can get up. In the last chapter of this book, I have described a class of people in whom personal egotism and ambitions have been largely subordinated to the civic sense: it is to such a band of workers that I look forward for delivering the urgent message in the remotest villages and towns of India. There are scores of intellectuals and hundreds of eager men and women whose urge for social service is being starved or frittered away for want of the right channels; if they could see the opportunity which the villages of the East Punjab and in fact of India offer them for quiet and efficient service they would not fail to seize the opportunity. Such volunteers cannot be conscripted, and I cannot help smiling when I think of the order of the East Punjab Government closing all schools and colleges for six months in the interest of 'refugee rehabilitation'; even the tiny tots in the elementary schools are perhaps required as volunteers, and somehow it is considered that hundreds and thousands of boys in the towns can at the same time be dumped into refugee camps under professors who cannot control the students even in the courtyard of the college. Then, the 'concessions' offered to the students by way of examination degrees and diplomas remind me of the baits (good food and clothes and pension) offered during the last war for recruitment. Rehabilitation work wants not conscripts but volunteers, and volunteers possessing in an abundant measure courage, conviction and faith. It is not necessary that every village be 'covered' from the outset; one thousand young men and women capably led could, in six months, introduce a leaven in the countryside which would stir it up beyond expectations. They should be as far as possible a mixed company: students, psychologists, economists, Red Cross workers, agricultural college graduates (or even undergraduates) and so on. They need not have elaborate equipment. Blackboards, pieces of chalk, copies of *Village Home Doctor* or some such book, a small medicine chest, a few books of devotional songs and folklore, an assured supply of the *Harijan*—and a football with a pump. Their entry into the village should not be like the invasion of the officials of the State whose approach causes a great commotion among chickens in the little poultry-farms and the village shops. Preferably, they should, literally and figuratively, infiltrate into the village. They are to come as friendly advisers, not as critics. The villager is no fool; he has experience in his own job which has been accumulated from generations, and in fact in his own primitive technique he has little to learn from the 'theorists' from the town. Like a child, the simple rustic mind trusts persons more than precepts; once the barriers of mistrust have broken down, the villager would be less loth to learn the new methods of farming or living which scientific knowledge has to offer him. The social workers will earn rich dividends on early patience; as time goes on they would receive trust and co-operation in increasing measure. They are not likely to be short of accommodation; their adult school could at a pinch be held under a *Pipal* tree; even the 'Visva-Bharati' occasionally holds its classes under the sky. Village 'gurdwaras' and temples and mosques will have larger attendance than ever before; after the recital of scriptures or prayers there will be prayer speeches of the unknown Gandhis from among the social workers. The keepers of the temples and 'gurdwaras' may be persuaded to function during their long idle hours as the store keepers of the village seed-stores. On a weekend there may be a friendly visit of a professor or an insurance agent from the neighbouring town to those townsmen who are engaged in this interesting experiment in the village. This traffic between the village and the town may have the happy result of diverting a professional doctor or a teacher from the uncertain quest for rich rewards in the town into a modest career in the village.

Concurrently with the presence of such a band of social workers in the villages, the Government could launch administrative and economic plans for agrarian reform—the first steps for increasing the productivity of the land, generally revitalizing and integrating the village economy in order to ensure a higher standard of life for the masses.

At this stage I would commend the adoption, with modifications to suit local conditions, of a plan outlined by Tarlok Singh in his book, *Poverty and Social Change.* His book, coming as it does from a student of economics with practical experience of revenue administration, cannot be summed up in any of the popular 'isms'; if his thesis must be classified, I would call it evolutionary democratic socialism. Tarlok Singh recognizes the evils of fragmentation of holdings: the uneconomic units of cultivation leave neither means nor incentive for the introduction of modern agricultural or technological aids to fertility. Nationalization is, however, rejected as an immediate policy, for it is opposed to the beliefs— or perhaps superstitions—of the farmer; co-operative farming by excluding the actual process of cultivation (as distinguished from the purchase of seeds and credit and sale of crops) from the sphere of co-operation omits the first essential steps for the development of agriculture. 'Joint Village Management' is proposed as the agency for running the economy of the village; it is something more than a 'Panchayat,' it is the primary adult electorate of the village functioning through various sub-committees. The vexed subject of uneconomic holdings is solved by recognizing the ownership of every owner, but for cultivation and harvests the land is vested in the 'Joint Village Management'. The arable land is to be divided into suitable units for a single family, or in some cases for groups of families. The broad rectangular or square fields for cultivation would be different from the jigsaw puzzle of ownership preserved in the revenue records; an ownership dividend will, however, continue to be paid to the owners who do not cultivate the land, but it would be only an equitable amount, which would not include the remuneration which properly belongs to the tiller of the soil. The village community will absorb part of its surplus hands after 'rationalization' of agriculture in village industries, notably dairy and poultry farming. Entering the market as a unit, the village would secure better prices for its increasing surpluses and would thus accumulate its own capital for purchase of fertilizers and machinery. Tarlok Singh even envisages investment by the 'Joint Village Management' in large-scale industrial enterprises which should prevent the concentration of wealth in the towns.

Tarlok Singh's plan has the merit of a patient and practical approach to a complicated problem. He takes the prejudices of the peasant into account. He also assumes a peaceful but fairly quick evolution, in preference to a violent revolution. In the transitional period he avoids the necessity of downright expropriation by a limited 'ownership dividend' to those who do not themselves till the soil. By separating the wages for work in the field from the remuneration for ownership of lands, he overcomes the difficult problem of maintaining or even increasing the incentive of an individualist economy in a corporate economy. In the 'Joint Village Management' is suggested an organic body which has scope for growth and which would take in as much as it can chew at a time. The waste and loss inevitable in petty farming and unorganized marketing are eliminated by the management of the agricultural processes of the entire village as a unit under a local authority. The landless labourer particularly stands to gain from service under the village organized as a unit rather than under the exacting hiring farmers or their scolding wives. The landless labourer may indeed achieve through the 'Joint Village Management' freedom not only from grinding poverty, but from the bondage of caste which at present is inextricably tied up with economic dependence. As for the artisans, they have a better chance for improving their technique if they are organized not merely for the service of the local village market but also for the neighbouring villages and are assured of the necessary capital and a certain market through a local authority.

The development of village industries is complementary to agrarian reform. Rationalization of agriculture, even without the introduction of power-farming which may come later, would release many people from the land which at present has too little work and too little food for all those who cling to it. To minds fed on the fabulous prosperity of America and the feats of factory manufacture in Western Europe, cottage industries may appear as a relic of the 'horse and buggy' era in the age of the motor car and the aeroplane. Discerning minds have, however, already seen the seamy side of the application of technology to industry; the lop-sided growth of mass-producing industries and the resultant centralization of productive power in a few centres under private or state capitalism have become a menace to the progress and even the existence of humanity. In his book, *Science, Liberty and Peace,* Aldous Huxley has analysed the social and political effects of applied science on large-scale agriculture and industry, and indicated how the development of centralized production jeopardizes the freedom of the individual and the peace of the world. The dispersal of industrial production and a wider distribution of the management and the profits of manufacture appear to be conditions precedent to the maintenance of individual liberty, and for the preservation of a democratic way of life, and for the prevention of jingoistic nationalism. Even from the narrower point of view of production there are many manufacturing processes which lend themselves to efficient management by small units. Ralph Barsodi's studies have shown that mass-producing and mass-distributing methods are suited technologically only to about one-third of the total production of goods; for the remaining two-thirds individuals or co-operating groups producing for subsistence and small markets can largely make up for the advantages of mass-production by economies in distribution. From the larger point of view—which is the point of view of the individual worker and his family—a life of reasonable comfort derived in familiar and wholesome surroundings from congenial occupations has a great deal to offer in terms of human relationships and happiness.

In the present state of India's development this debate on the first principles of production is somewhat premature. Even if mass-production in huge plants were the only alternative, India has now neither the capital nor the technical skill to set up such plants. Even a dozen Bombay Plans will not in any measurable time bring our country to a stage of industrial progress when cottage industries may be confined to toy making. Our factories will hardly absorb the natural increase in population in the towns and the surplus labour released by rationalized agriculture. Meanwhile the same eighty per cent of the country's population in the villages must have a by-occupation, partly as an insurance against a failure of or damage to the crops from natural causes, and partly to fill in the idle months of the year and the idle hours of the day. In the interest of national production itself, during the next few years it is imperative to satisfy many of the basic requirements of the village within the village itself. Domestic industries may mean for single individuals a relatively small addition to their incomes but against the background of the very low *per capita* income even this increment to the national dividend cannot be ignored. There is, moreover, no justification for regarding cottage industries as arrested forms of industrial development; there is nothing static about handlooms, spinning wheels and the small and simple machines used in 'domestic' manufacture. The Lancashire looms of the eighteenth-century did not have a tithe of the productivity of the present-day textile factories in the same region. It is not impossible that the productivity of the small-scale producer through improvement of his tools and the supply of cheap power may, within its own limits, similarly increase. Superficial observers ridicule Gandhiji for his advocacy of hand-spinning and the 'charkha' (spinning wheel) is represented as a symbol of his rejection of the machine. Gandhiji is, however, not opposed to the machine as such; the 'charkha' itself is a machine, though a simple one. Gandhiji did not just adopt the 'charkha'; he improved upon it; hand-spinning was not treated as an old-wives' recipe but a scientific process amenable to careful observation and creative improvement. The 'Yeravda Charkha' or the 'Magan Charkha' is as different from the primitive 'charkha' which my grandmother used to ply as the newest Rolls Royce car from the earliest cars. Gandhiji's active approach has been adopted by the All India Village Industries Association in fostering other village industries; the full exploitation of the existing technique, the avoidance of waste, the improvement of the quality of the produce and the progressive improvement of the technique. Some of the village industries, particularly the processing of home-grown food, have not only an economic aspect, they have also a bearing on national health. Hand-pounding of unpolished rice and hand-grinding of wheat flour may appear crude processes but the product carries the full approbation of authorities on dietetics like Sir Robert McCarrison since it retains the full nutritive value of food by saving valuable vitamins and mineral salts from the destruction which is inevitable in the machine-processing of the foodstuffs. Similarly, village-made *gur* and village-pressed oil have more nutritive value than the articles turned out by the factories and, in any case, their place in the national economy cannot be underrated particularly when the industrial potential of our country is not very high. The improvement of hand-made paper and tanning industries has been encouraging under an intelligent direction from the All India Village Industries Association. Simple, economical and practical methods of disposal of carcasses in the villages have systematized the tanning industries. 'Carcasses are now removed with care and flayed in such a way as to avoid unnecessary cuts; every part of the dead animal is put to some use. From the flesh, glue is made, while the entrails and the intestines are converted into guts. The fat can be used for lubricating and industrial purposes and manure is obtainable from the powder made out of the bulls' flesh and bones. Both bones and horns are suitable material for the manufacture of articles of daily use, such as combs, hair pins, knife or umbrella handles. Chrome tanning has also been developed into a cottage industry.' When I read this paragraph in V. L. Mehta's article on 'Village Industries' in that historic volume, *Gandhiji: His Life and Work,* I could not help recalling a passage on the by-products of the large-scale meat industry of Chicago which used to illustrate the economics of large-scale factory production in our college texbooks on Economics. There are economies in small-scale production as well as large-scale production. Scientists need not take small-sized production units as a parody of applied science; they themselves have in the past been tempted by the great rewards from big business to concentrate on the enlargement and improvement of massive manufacturing plants. With a little more attention from applied science, the productivity of cottage industries can be increased by improvement of the tools and the provision of cheap power from wind, water and the sun. The lure of 'Atomic Research,' may not blur the imperative immediate needs of our present productive units, large or small. Scientific laboratories should be at the disposal not only of Big Business (with capital B) but of the small producer; the former's terms may be better but the latter's importance in national economy is not less. A balanced economy for India needs the co-ordination of the agricultural improvements with village industries and of the village economy with that of the town.

In this process the town owes a long-standing debt to the village. During the last fifty years the exodus from the village to the town has been continuous. There was nothing unnatural in this exodus; indeed, one may wonder why it was not greater than it was, since the pressure on land has been increasing and there is not enough land to go round. 'Back to the village' is certainly a retrograde slogan if it implies a reverse flow of population from the town to the village; 'Away to the town' may be a more appropriate summons.

Unfortunately, however, the emigrants from the village to the town during the last half a century included the most enterprising elements with whose departure life in the village began to wither. Backwardness in the slang of the town has become synonymous with the word 'rural' and the typical left-handed compliment from one urbanite to another urbanite is 'you ignorant villager!' This silly snobbery signifies the walls which divide the village from the town. In each generation the village was denuded of its ambitious and adventurous elements and those who could have helped to create amenities of life in the village set out to seek them in the town. Such gaps between town and village in talent and wealth, career and opportunity, were unjust to the village but also unprofitable to the town, since the standard of thinking and living of eighty per cent of people must ultimately govern the limits of prosperity or happiness of the whole nation. Gandhiji from the first saw the glaring contradiction in India's economy, and he has missed no opportunity of driving it home. He persuaded the Indian National Congress to hold its sessions in the village; the venue was symbolic of the importance of the village in the national fabric; it was the townsmen who went to the village to attend the Congress and not the villagers who were to trudge to the town for the occasion. Whether it is education or nature cure, Gandhiji wants to know if it would suit the village or not; he shocked naturopaths by suggesting to them to locate their clinics in villages. In his dress and mode of life he has completely identified himself with the poverty and nakedness of the lowliest. It would appear, however, that the Mahatma's rural abode, like his loin cloth, has become a commonplace to his devout followers; and to the educated urbanite, Sevagram Ashram may even appear as a necessary retreat from visitors, press correspondents and blood pressure. To Gandhiji himself, his residence in the village may be a sacred duty; to some it may appear an act of asceticism. Rural life has, however, its *raison d'etre* at more worldly levels as well. The pleasures of the countryside attract townsmen all over the world; those who can afford may have their country houses, others have the public highways and public resorts for hikes and holidays. The weekend in a suburb or in the country has been a recipe for keeping statesmen going. For all I know, Pt. Nehru and Sardar Patel may already have selected sites for their country cottages at a motorable distance from Delhi; and until the cottages are put up they may make provisional arrangements with Dr. Zakir Hussain for weekends in Okhla. In the West, many men prominent in public life have, after their retirement, enjoyed an 'agricultural' old age; as I think of the British statesman Lord Townshend, who is remembered in the eighteenth-century history as 'Turnip Townshend,' I begin to wonder how many of our ministers will be known to posterity with such prefixes as potato, cabbage, or soyabean.

A General cannot efficiently wage a war in the desert from his armchair in the General Headquarters; he must stay in the front theatre, if not in the front line. No more can a minister direct rural rehabilitation from

Simla or Jullundur; he must be in the thick of the battle, which is none the less serious because people slowly die of starvation or cold rather than of bullet shots. A General by his presence in the front line does not physically contribute to the capture of any outpost, but he learns from personal observation and association with his men something which may help him to plan his entire strategy. A minister in a village can exercise the same moral influence as a General in the trenches; he encourages, cheers and inspires those who need encouragement, cheer and inspiration. I like to think that the ministers of the East Punjab Government, by a self-denying ordinance, would order the district magistrates to derequisition their official summer residences in Simla and winter residences in Jullundur, and shift to a ministers' dormitory in the Secretariat building from where they would branch off from their periodical Cabinet meetings and occasional tours to their respective headquarters in various villages which should eventually bear their names as the monuments of their constructive work. Some executive officers of the Ferozepore district were recently posted at 'tehsil' headquarters, but this admirable step was forced by the Sutlej river which had pulled down the official residences in the September floods; it needed a flood to enforce a policy which is equally in the interest of the administration—of those who administer and of those who are administered.

So far I have been discussing the problems of rehabilitation in the villages, where the vast majority of the uprooted immigrants from the West Punjab have to be settled. There are, however, a good one million refugees who made their living from trade, banking, manufacture and other professions, all of which are at present concentrated in the towns. The rehabilitation of the town-dwellers is a difficult problem; while the cultivators of land can be allotted a given number of acres for a fresh start, it is not possible to divide one-fifth of a shop or one-fiftieth of a factory or a hypothetical percentage of professional work among the refugees. The local population of the East Punjab towns has the typical townsman's double-faced attitude; it may be kind-hearted but it is also hard-headed. Lip sympathy is of no consequence to those who are in desperate search of a shelter and a living; it is a strange reflection on the inconsistency of human beings that those very people who distribute free rations at railway stations or public squares on the first day of the arrival of the refugees, rack-rent them for accommodation and recover extortionate prices for wheat, sugar and cloth. Those who are already entrenched in trade and the professions, in spite of effusive sympathy for the privations of the refugees, cannot easily bring themselves to share their custom with the newcomers. And the newcomers do not find it easy to turn to another profession or learn a new trade; the pull of the familiar occupation remains and the contempt for manual labour was not in most cases lost with personal belongings. Most of the Muslim evacuees from the East Punjab were cultivators, manual workers and artisans; and the proportion of those who lived by trade and the professions was small. The West Punjab refugees have to grasp this fact. It is a common complaint in the towns of the East Punjab that while there are any number of people prepared to work as managers òr clerks there are few offering as artisans, factory operatives or manual workers. A hundred persons would like to peddle a basket of vegetables at every street corner of the towns, but even a handsome wage does not attract a labourer or a cartman to assist in carrying the vegetables to the market, and few farmers are anxious to grow vegetables. The inelasticity of the supply for certain occupations such as that of petty trader or banker will eventually force some of their numerous practitioners to take a turning. There is a real need for doctors and teachers in the villages even though the immediate rewards may be poor. As for businessmen, entrepreneurs, bankers and industrialists, the West Punjab possessed an exceptional reserve of talent, which built up the credit, the trade and the industry of the province and if the East Punjab cannot immediately absorb it, it would be an asset to other provinces. Other provinces will, however, welcome refugees from the West Punjab only when they are assured that by resettling the refugees they would not be unsettling the peace.

Chapter XII

A New Outlook

In an earlier chapter, I discussed the problem of mental rehabilitation of the refugees; the school of adversity has its own lessons for those who have the will and the capacity to learn from it. To be dispassionate is not necessarily to be dehumanized; coolness of mind does not follow from coldness of heart; sympathy is something different from pity. A person, with a sense of history, when faced with a national crisis, is less concerned with naming the criminals on the spot than with the understanding of the underlying causes of the crisis and the short-term as well as long-term measures for its cure. Religious persecution is not a new phenomenon; that it should occur again and again is not because history like an idiot repeats itself, but because the human race fails to learn from its blunders which punctuate the pages of history. 'The greatest lesson of history,' says Huxley, 'is that nobody wants to learn from history'. If this were not so, religious intolerance could not have raised its head in the twentieth-century India. Destiny has played many a cruel jest on those who decimated or drove out their religious minorities. Those zealous Catholics who massacred Admiral Coligny and his fellow Huguenots on the St. Bartholomew's Day did not know that they had deprived France of some of her best seamen, who could have helped her in the race with England for the command of the seas. James I and Charles I of England were not sorry to see members of that troublsome sect, the Puritans, set sail for America; they thought it was a good riddance. The Pilgrim Fathers who were dismissed as failures in the old world became the architects of a new one; their colonies, brought into being by the double quest for liberty of individual conscience and economic opportunity, set a pattern for the political and economic evolution of the North American Continent, and eventually exercised a tremendous influence on the history of the world. In our own time the Nazis facilitated the regimentation of the German people by making a scapegoat of the Jews; the political value of this policy was offset by the lowering of moral standards, and the effects of the expulsion of Jewish scientists on German war-potential were seen in the last stages of the war; in his last hectic days in the Berlin Chancellery, Adolf Hitler may have rued the day when he decided to extirpate or scare away the non-Aryan scientists, whose researches helped America and Britain and thus made the fatal difference between victory and defeat.

A realist is not a person who has a hazy memory of yesterday and no plans for the morrow. What is true for an individual is truer for a nation; a proper perspective in the present is impossible without peeping into the vista of the past and seeking the vision of the future. For me, one of the most disheartening things in the tragedy of the Punjab has been the absence of a proper perspective except at the very top of the national life. It would have been too much to expect from the majority of the sufferers themselves that they would suddenly attain objectivity after experiencing physical and mental shocks. Yet, there is a certain section of opinion-making people, teachers, scientists, publicists, from whom a certain amount of objectivity is—or at least should be—expected. If in the months of August and September a critical observer could overhear the conversation of these gentlemen and ladies in their drawing rooms or offices, in most cases the opinions expressed would have been indistinguishable from those of the refugees themselves or our Yellow Press which gives the reader full value for two annas in the glaring headlines only. For many people, there was an irresistible temptation to arrange little debates in which the ministers or the political leaders had the worst of it. One should have expected that the crisis would evoke an active constructive reaction to the tasks of reconstruction, but these humdrum tasks were probably considered the business of Nehru and Neogy, Patel and Ayyangar. I am not belittling the efforts of those who voluntarily came forward to do their share of work, to serve in the refugee camps, to donate bread and blankets, to tend the sick and the wounded, but I believe that there is among our intelligentsia a large number of men and women who have either not grasped the full magnitude of the disaster or failed to see their particular immediate roles in meeting it. There is work enough for all those who would volunteer to come to the East Punjab's villages and towns—for engineers who would build houses and roads with the available materials or design cheap multi-purpose furniture; for doctors who would open little portable dispensaries; for scientists who would condescend to use applied science for restarting and improving small industries in villages and small towns; for statisticians who would collect figures from fields and factories; for economists who desire to work out theories from a hard reality and to experiment in Collective Farming or 'Joint Village Management'. These small and immediate tasks have nothing heroic about them, but they cannot be neglected in the hope of miraculous results from Master Plans to be framed, financed, and followed up through the agency of the State. During the British rule, many Indians hoped for too little from the Government; now they hope for too much. And political controversy appears to survive in a form which suited a period of struggle for freedom, but is already out of date in a period of reconstruction. Poverty, disease or hunger cannot be scared away by agitation alone. In the past political subjection prevented our growth, but political freedom only supplies the background for progress through discipline, organization and diligence of the people. Political freedom is like air; you cannot live without it, but you cannot live on it either.

A secular, national and progressive outlook alone can help a people to realize the full benefits of political freedom. There is no necessary connection between political freedom and a progressive democratic regime. The high hopes pinned on nationalism in the nineteenth-century and even after the First World War have been belied by experience: it was not too long a step from Garibaldi to Mussolini. Political traditions are of slow growth in congenial soil. After the First World War, President Wilson thought that the American constitution could be transplanted in Central and South-Eastern Europe, but except in Czechoslovakia (which imbibed the spirit as well as the institutions of democracy) Central and South-Eastern Europe reverted to autocratic or oligarchic rule, the democratic facade notwithstanding.

It is to be fervently hoped that national freedom and a progressive socialist-democracy will go together in Asian countries which are breaking the shackles of foreign imperialism. One cannot, however, disguise a feeling of disappointment at lost opportunities. In the Middle East there are several independent States but quite a few of them are weighed down by the dead-weight of the past. In China, the tradition of Sun Yat-sen survives, but so does the tradition of the feudal warlord; the national unity of China has been irreparably rent by an unending civil war. In Indonesia, the uprising against foreign domination has given rise to a surging nationalism, and in Burma British rule is formally at an end. The assassination of Burma's leader U Aung San and his colleagues in Rangoon was, however, an omen for Asia: it pointed to the real danger of political violence which years ago effectively put an end to individual freedom and parliamentary democracy in Japan.

Against this background it is only natural that both the East and the West should look up to India for giving a lead to the rest of Asia in building national unity, a free democracy and economic prosperity. Leaders of Burma, Indonesia, Ceylon and other Asian countries have expressed their hopes in the moral and political leadership of India in Asia; not all of these compliments may be brushed away as courteous compliments from sister nations. I, for one, share these hopes but my reasons may be slightly different from those of many of my countrymen. My faith in a national, secular and democratic India does not wholly or even largely derive from India's past history. I am proud of India's cultural heritage, but I am painfully aware of the centrifugal tendencies in her political history which through endless centuries made her a prey to anarchy or invasion. Political unity and national loyalty are comparatively recent phenomena; they were first practised by European nations. Culturally, India has had from early times a fundamental unity from Kashmir to Cape Comorin, but politically she remained disparate. It was the ambition of every king and princeling of ancient India to become a lord of the universe, a *Chakravarti*. The Rajput princes carried on their interminable vendetta against the neighbouring 'rajas' for some point of honour, a fancied insult, or a face. During Muslim rule it was customary for 'princes royal' to rebel against the monarch if he took an unconscionable time in dying; the governors of provinces, the 'nizams' and the 'nawabs' declared themselves independent sovereigns in outlying provinces whenever communications with the capital or chaos in the palace made the step a militarily feasible proposition. The idea that Rajagopalachari should declare himself independent, as the Maharajadhiraja of Bengal, and found a 'Chari Dynasty' may appear indescribably funny, but such events were common from the twelfth to the eighteenth-century until the British took over.

My faith in India's capacity to lead the rest of Asia in working out a democratic and progressive national state is derived not from ancient and mediaeval periods of Indian history, but from the events in the last thirty years, from the nature of the nationalist movement and the calibre of the leaders who led the fight for political freedom. A recent British writer on India, F.G. Griffiths, a former leader of the European Group in the Central Legislature, has suggested that 'it would eventually be realized that Mr. Gandhi made democracy unworkable in India'. It is usual for most Western writers to smile at Gandhiji's curious mixture of saint and statesman, and his attempt at 'moralizing' politics. The Machiavellian tradition has been so strong in the Western intellect that a mention of morality in politics is a red rag to it. Gandhiji's morality is not a set of abstract dogmas; it is a series of principles which no theorist on democracy could discard. That it is possible to differ without hatred, to fight tyranny without killing the tyrant, to solve differences by discussion without resort to violence; that politics are not immune from the ethics of civilized society; that even good political ends do not justify bad means; that political power is derived from the people and is to be held in trust for them—these beliefs of Gandhiji are not opposed to modern democracy, which, in fact, cannot survive without practising them to a greater or lesser degree.

To say that Gandhiji by importing religion into politics contributed to the growth of political communalism is to betray an ignorance of the nature of his emphasis on religion; he emphasized and still emphasizes the unity of all religions; his evening prayer epitomizes this unity; his prayer speeches translate this unity in terms of everyday life. Gandhiji's religious approach was inherent in his own personality; but it is arguable that an anti-religious or non-religious approach to the Indian masses would not have cut ice with them. One can sum up parliamentary democracy before a British audience by saying that 'politics is a game where you may bowl your opponent out according to the rules of the game, but you are not permitted to blow out his brains'; but the Indian people could better understand the same thesis when Gandhiji preached to them that one could convert one's opponent but not kill him. Secularism in politics can be attained by completely eschewing religion or by realizing the true religious spirit. India has had recently an excess of religiosity, not of religion. The division of India was not forced by a religious movement but by those politicians who could exploit the name of religion and the fear of economic exploitation; Pakistan was a paradise not for men of religion, but for ambitious politicians, businessmen and officials, where they could rule without the shadow of Hindu competition.

Even during the fight with the British for political freedom, non-violence was to many people a policy and not a creed as it has been to Gandhiji. After the end of the British rule, many people may be tempted to relegate non-violence to the limbo of discarded theories. Its application in the international field would appear a utopian ideal to the majority of politicians and publicists all over the world, though the technological advances in instruments of war-making leave no alternative to non-violence. In the national field and in the tasks of reconstruction non-violence in its true sense is not a theory but an urgent necessity; it is the greatest safeguard for democracy and individual freedom. When there is a tradition for people not to break the heads of their opponents, government by free discussion is facilitated; when minorities are not to be chased out or smothered with castor oil or the fear of physical violence they have a chance to speak out and be heard. Non-violence, if correctly understood, may save India not only from communal strife, but also from the tyranny of straitjackets of political or economic 'systems' which are forcibly put on men of flesh and blood for the glory of their makers.

There is one contribution of Gandhiji to India which should be an asset of inestimable value to her future progress. It is his ideal of public service without desire for personal profit or power. It is not a new idea; Christ and Buddha preached it; the Bible and the *Bhagawad Gita* taught it. The Franciscan Order was based on it, and Pierre Ceresole's international work camps in our own time practised it. Yet no individual before Gandhiji had extended its application to the 'game of politics'. In himself he exemplified a frank rejection of wealth and formal attributes of power; by association with him grew up scores of leaders and thousands of comparatively unknown men and women who learnt to serve their country without the common incentives. The fight for freedom called for renunciation from those who did not perhaps believe in renunciation; prisons strengthened the moral fibre, and the infectious humility of Gandhiji saved many leaders from that pride and ambition which make fighters in political battles poor leaders in peace time. Gandhiji has not changed all or even most of his followers; there are Congressmen who probably have gone on making money and seeking political power all the time; but there is a hopeful nucleus of talented men and women who are not driven by the double motor of profit and power, who seem to be self-propelled and in fact are propelled by a sense of duty. This nucleus must grow until it covers not only the national leaders but leaders of public opinion and public servants in the provinces and districts and villages. On this growth of public spirit rests the reconstruction of the East Punjab today and of the rest of India tomorrow. This subordination of the individual's interest to the welfare of the community cannot be cultivated wholesale or all at once. Even at the best of times only a minority can be indoctrinated with it and this minority includes writers, journalists, politicians, ministers, civil servants—all those who are the vocal upper crust on a passive majority and whose careers should have a significance over and above the material rewards they obtain.

Chapter XIII

Postscript

This book was in the press when, on 30th January, Mahatma Gandhi was assassinated. A postscript to this survey of the riots and rehabilitation in the Punjab would be in line with the universal stock-taking which the tragedy in New Delhi has evoked.

The last few months of Gandhiji's life and the manner of his death constituted an epic struggle between an all-embracing humanism and sectarian fanaticism. Nearly a quarter of a century ago he wrote, 'I see no way of achieving anything in this afflicted country without a lasting heart-unity between Hindus and Mussalmans of India. I believe in the immediate possibility of achieving it, because it is so natural, so necessary for both and because I believe in human nature'. He knew that lasting unity could not be forged by percentages and pacts and when he offered 'blank cheques', his contempt for the methods of the market-place was implicit in the offer. He knew and felt in his everyday life the ties uniting the various communities in the land. Invariably he emphasized the points of contact rather than those of divergence. When the Muslim League froze its political programme in the mould of Pakistan, and demanded partition of the country as a solution of the communal problem, Gandhiji was indefatigable in his pleading for unity and tolerance. Vivisection of India hurt him because it vivisected his own heart, which would not accept partitions of political geography. When he called the partition of India a sin, his reaction was emotional. Yet his emotional reactions had a deeper insight than the syllogisms of logical lawyers. He understood the human factor in India as nobody else did. He knew the havoc a separatist movement could work with the masses of this subcontinent. He feared that the division of India based on the assumption of an essential incompatibility between the two major communities would stereotype communal bitterness, intolerance and warfare.

The partition of India was at last a settled fact: it was part of the deed of transfer of power from Britain to India, and an agreed decision between the Congress and the League. This was a bitter blow to Gandhiji. 'The British Parliament would make two nations of India, by passing a bill about the division of India in Parliament. What is there to gloat over in the tragedy? Was this to be a parting shot of the British?' These words addressed to a prayer gathering on 29th June, 1947, expressed his anguish. He did not share the delusion of the Muslim League and the illusion of the Congress that the partition of the country would suddenly restore communal harmony. His hand as ever was on the pulse of the people. The fever of communal hatred artificially stimulated in recent years was still raging. While top-ranking politicians exchanged messages of goodwill in the press and hoped that the two communities and the two States would henceforth be good neighbours, Gandhiji, less optimistic but more vigilant, set himself to the task of mitigating the immediate dangers of partition. The remaining months of his life were devoted to the ending of the chronic feud between the communities, and to ensuring that this feud did not transform itself into an antagonism between the two sister States created by the partition of the country.

The formal transfer of power from Britain to India took place on 15th August, 1947. The architect of Indian Independence was not in Delhi to receive the homage of the populace. The ship of freedom after a hazardous voyage had come into port, but the Captain considered a little cleaning up in the engine room immediately more important than bouquets and banquets. Gandhiji's decision to stay in Calcutta during the critical days of transition was highly prescient; by throwing his own frail body between communal passion and peace, he prevented Calcutta and Bengal from going the way of Lahore and the Punjab.

Meanwhile, the Punjab volcano had exploded. Violence or fear of violence had driven the minorities to flee across the border; the process was already too far gone by the time Gandhiji was in a position to leave Calcutta. His plans for tour of the Punjab were upset by the disturbances in Delhi. The paralysis of Delhi was a derivation from, and indeed an extension of, the paralysis of the Punjab; if this creeping sickness was to be halted Delhi needed his immediate attention. The Mahatma decided 'to do or die' at Delhi. He 'did' at Delhi: he was able to awaken the conscience of Delhi's citizens. But he also died at Delhi.

If Gandhiji had been in Lahore in mid-August, could he have halted the Punjab's race downhill? This will remain a question mark in the recent history of this subcontinent. There was plenty of inflammable material in the Punjab: the disappearance of a composite though corrupt ministry, the memories of the March atrocities in the Western Punjab, the existence of communal armies and warfare, particularly in Lahore and Amritsar, the violent impact of the idea of the division of the country upon the minds of the majority and minority communities, the psychological havoc wrought by the provisional partition of the province, the necessary dissolution of the administration for communal regrouping at the very time it was needed most, and finally, in the background of it all, the seven years' campaign for the division of the country which shook the very sense of preservation of the people and severed neighbourly bonds and common humanity. These were very heavy odds, but Gandhiji had overcome similar hurdles at Calcutta. In the critical days of the transition the balance of communal forces was precarious; it tilted in the Punjab in favour of anarchy with the sheer weight of the past, but it turned in favour of peace at Calcutta when tipped by Gandhiji's presence. If the leaders of public opinion, particularly Sikh leaders in the East Punjab and Muslim leaders in the West Punjab, had maintained the necessary vigilance, events might have taken a different course. If communal anarchy is infectious, so is communal harmony. Continued peace in Calcutta in the months of August and September 1947 led to the general easing of the situation in the East as well as the West Bengal. Anarchy in Lahore and Amritsar, on the other hand, engulfed the East as well as the West Punjab, spreading as far as Delhi at one end and Karachi at the other.

Gandhiji's role in localizing and extinguishing communal conflict was unique. There was no greater policeman in history; he restored order, not with truncheon and gun, but by exhorting, admonishing and warning those who had gone off the rails. His objectivity amidst general excitement was superb. He put the merits of peace above the balance sheet of rights and wrongs. He exhorted the Hindus to be just to the Muslim minority in the Indian Union irrespective of what was done in Pakistan. And by peace he meant not the absence of physical violence, but the union of hearts between friends and neighbours and compatriots. Many Hindus and Sikhs believed that Gandhiji was advocating one-sided forgiveness, and that he was partial to the Muslim minority. At the other end, for years he had been vilified as the arch-enemy of Muslims. After his death, he was described by his erstwhile Muslim opponents in India and Pakistan as the greatest friend and protector of Muslims. It was not Gandhiji who had changed, but the mood of different sects and parties. As for him, if he had any partiality, it was for peace and for the common man of this subcontinent.

His death removed the greatest living barrier against communalism on this subcontinent, but through the violent impact of the tragedy on the mind of this generation, a barrier quite as powerful as his life may arise phoenix-like from his ashes. Gandhi dead may be more powerful than Gandhi alive.

The refugees from Western Pakistan who were sometimes bewildered by Gandhiji's exhortations for restraint, patience and forgiveness have been hit the hardest by his death. So long as he was holding communal passions at bay, he could not devote himself whole-heartedly to the task of rehabilitation. The fine response of Delhi to his last fast freed him to think about invigorating the organizations engaged in constructive work. His blueprint for the reorganization of the National Congress for furthering the tempo of constructive activity was taking shape in his mind, when the assassin's bullets put an abrupt end to these plans. I have no doubt that rehabilitation of the uprooted Punjab would have received a high priority from him. Rehabilitation meant to him the restoration of the refugees to their homes; this was a task beset with innumerable obstacles, but after his death there is no individual in this subcontinent who could even attempt the task. In the narrower sense rehabilitation will go on: the allotment of land and houses, plans of agricultural or industrial development and absorption of the refugees in useful employment in the provinces or districts of adoption. Yet even in this process, the country would miss one who was a unique arbiter between the people and the Government. No other individual could at once rebuke the refugees, criticize the bureaucracy and pull up the ministers for their lapses. The greatest rebel against the Government in British India was in free India the greatest buffer between the Government and the people.

Index

Printed in Great Britain
by Amazon

36279530R00106